LUFTWAFFE IN COMBAT 1939-45

Me. 262
STORMBIRD ASCENDING

BOB CARRUTHERS

Pen & Sword
AVIATION

This edition published in 2013 by
Pen & Sword Aviation
An imprint of
Pen & Sword Books Ltd
47 Church Street
Barnsley
South Yorkshire
S70 2AS

First published in Great Britain in 2012 in digital format by
Coda Books Ltd.

ISBN 978 1 78159 231 1

A CIP catalogue record for this book is
available from the British Library

Printed and bound by CPI Group (UK) Ltd, Croydon, CR0 4YY

Pen & Sword Books Ltd incorporates the Imprints of Pen & Sword Aviation, Pen & Sword Family History, Pen & Sword Maritime, Pen & Sword Military, Pen & Sword Discovery, Pen & Sword Politics, Pen & Sword Atlas, Pen & Sword Archaeology, Wharncliffe Local History, Wharncliffe True Crime, Wharncliffe Transport, Pen & Sword Select, Pen & Sword Military Classics, Leo Cooper, The Praetorian Press, Claymore Press, Remember When, Seaforth Publishing and Frontline Publishing

For a complete list of Pen & Sword titles please contact
PEN & SWORD BOOKS LIMITED
47 Church Street, Barnsley, South Yorkshire, S70 2AS, England
E-mail: enquiries@pen-and-sword.co.uk
Website: www.pen-and-sword.co.uk

CONTENTS

INTRODUCTION

This book forms part of the series entitled 'Hitler's War Machine.' The aim is to provide the reader with a varied range of materials drawn from original writings covering the strategic, operational and tactical aspects of the battles of Hitler's war on land and in the air. The concept behind the series is to provide the well-read and knowledgeable reader with an interesting compilation of related primary sources and the best of what is in the public domain to build a picture of a particular aspect of that titanic struggle.

I am pleased to report that the series has been well received and it is a pleasure to be able to bring original primary sources to the attention of an interested readership. I particularly enjoy discovering new primary sources, and I am pleased to be able to present them unadorned and unvarnished to a sophisticated audience. The primary sources such as Der Adler magazine, speak for themselves and the readership I strive to serve is the increasingly well informed community of reader/historians which needs no editorial lead and can draw its own conclusions. I am well aware that our community is constantly striving to discover new nuggets of information, and I trust that with this volume I have managed to stimulate fresh enthusiasm and that at least some of these facts and articles will be new to you and will provoke readers to research further down these lines of investigation, and perhaps cause established views to be challenged once more. I am aware at all times in compiling these materials that our relentless pursuit of more and better historical information is at the core our common passion. I trust that this selection will contribute to that search and will help all of us to better comprehend and understand the bewildering events of the last century.

In order to produce an interesting compilation giving a flavour of events at the tactical and operational level I have returned once more to the US Intelligence series of pamphlets and interviews, which contain an intriguing series of contemporary articles on weapons and tactics. I find this series of pamphlets particularly fascinating as they are written in the present tense and, as such, provide us with a sense of what was happening at the face of battle as events unfolded.

To complete the selection I have drawn upon a small section of the post war debriefs undertaken for the US Army Historical department. This is a hugely underrated source and is often overlooked. I have included them here as they give an excellent flavour of the frustrations experienced by pilots in the air commanders at the operational level attempting to make things work against a background of constant interference from Hitler.

Thank you for buying this small volume, it is intended to serve as an introduction to this legendary aircraft gathering together the best primary sources as well as the best of what is now in the public domain, we hope you enjoy this title and will go on to collect others in the series.

Bob Carruthers

Edinburgh 2012

THE MESSERSCHMITT Me.262

The popular misconception is often circulated that the Me.262 could somehow have made a major difference to the outcome of World War II had it not been for Hitler's insistence that it be utilised as a fighter-bomber.

In reality the Me.262 programme suffered from so many teething problems with the Jumo-004 engines that there was no real prospect of the Me.262 affecting the outcome of the war in any meaningful way. Hitler's insistence on development of the aircraft as a "Jabo" (meaning fighter-bomber) led to a bureaucratic fiasco, but it was not something which would have made a material difference to the outcome of the war.

Taking the flying characteristics of the aircraft into consideration, it may well be that the idea of using the Me.262 in the "Jabo" role was not so stupid at all. Hitler felt, with good reason in November 1943 that existing aircraft types could deal with Allied bombers. For this reason Hitler envisioned the Me.262 as an offensive ground-attack/bomber rather than a defensive interceptor. The configuration of a high speed, light payload Schnellbomber ("Fast Bomber") was intended to penetrate enemy airspace during the expected Allied invasion of France. His edict resulted in the development of (and concentration on) the Sturmvogel variant which was a Schnellbomber. It is debatable to what extent Hitler's interference extended the delay in bringing the Schwalbe into operation.

Hitler's major strategic concern was to be able to deal with Allied amphibious landings on the beachhead where they were most vulnerable. The Me. 262 was at its best in level flight, the twists and turns of a dogfight were too much for the prototype

The Messerschmitt Me.262

engines. Had there had been substantial quantities of jet bombers available it is possible that they could indeed have penetrated the thick fighter screen over the Normandy beachhead, they just might have made a difference; but the prospect seems slim.

In any event Hitler rejected arguments that the aircraft would be more effective as a fighter against Allied bombers systematically destroying the cities of Germany, and wanted it as a bomber for revenge attacks. According to Speer, Hitler felt its superior speed compared to other fighters of the era meant it could not be attacked and so preferred it for high altitude straight flying. The Sturmvogel was too "clean" for dive-bombing attacks; it would build up too much speed, becoming uncontrollable. It had no bombsight for performing horizontal bombing attacks from medium or high altitudes, but a skilled pilot could use it to perform useful horizontal attacks at low level, particularly with cluster munitions that didn't have to be aimed precisely.

Me.262 Origins

Despite sporadic official interest it was clear that the jet was the propulsion system of the future, German companies were working on combat aircraft based on the new turbojet engines. Following the flight tests of the He-178, in the autumn of 1939

Me.262 taken circa 1945

Heinkel began serious development of an operational fighter, the "He-280", which was to be powered by twin improved Heinkel engines and is discussed below.

Even before this, in the fall of 1938, a Messerschmitt design team under Dr. Waldermar Voight had drawn up concepts for an interceptor fighter with twin turbojet engines. The preliminary designs for "Project 1065", as it was designated, went through an iteration or two and finally resulted in a proposal submitted to the RLM in May 1940.

Messerschmitt's dream fighter had the turbojets mounted in nacelles under the middle of the wings. The wings were slightly swept to ensure proper center of gravity, and had an unusually thin wing for good high-speed performance. Since the wing's features for high-speed performance compromised low-speed handling, a "slat" was added to the front of the outer wings. The slat was automatically extended to improve handling at low speeds. The fuselage had a triangular cross section and substantial fuel capacity to feed the thirsty engines. The aircraft fully retractable tail wheel landing gear. In July 1940, the RLM ordered three prototypes, under the designation "Messerschmitt 262 (Me.262)", to be powered by BMW-003 engines.

Airframe development far outpaced engine development, and so the first prototype, the "Me.262-V1" ("V" standing for "Versuchs / Experimental"), was fitted with a single Jumo-210G piston engine with 530 kW (710 HP) and a two-bladed propeller for preliminary test flights. First flight was on 18 April 1941. The RLM was becoming more interested in the aircraft, ordering five more prototypes in July 1941, to follow the initial order for three.

The Me.262-V1 was finally fitted with a pair of BMW-003 turbojets, each with 5.40 kN (550 kgp / 1,200 lbf) thrust, in November 1941. The Jumo 210G piston engine was retained, which was fortunate, since the turbojet engines were hopelessly unreliable. On 25 March 1942, Messerschmitt test pilot Fritz Wendel took off and suffered immediate failures of both turbojets. He managed to make a go-round on the piston engine and land, damaging the aircraft but suffering no injury himself.

Development of the BMW-003 engine was progressing slowly while work on the Junkers Jumo-004 seemed more promising, and so the third prototype, the "Me.262-V3", was fitted with two Jumo-004A pre-production engines with 8.24 kN (840 kgp / 1,850 lbf) thrust each. Wendel took the V3 into the air on 18 July 1942 and found the aircraft extremely impressive. Unfortunately, the V3 prototype was wrecked on its second test flight, three weeks later.

The Me.262V-2 prototype, also powered by Jumo-004As, was not delivered until 2 October 1942. Despite all the delays and problems, the RLM had already ordered 15 preproduction Me.262s in May 1942, and added 30 more to the order that October. The He-280 was inferior in performance and the Me.262 was clearly the better option, but there was still no commitment to put the Me.262 into full production.

The RLM was vacillating between production of the Me.262

and the "Me-209", and an improved version of the piston-powered Messerschmitt Bf-109 fighter. The head of the RLM, Erhard Milch, was conservative and favoured the Me-209 over the much more radical Me.262. However, in the spring of 1943 the tide began to shift towards the jet fighter. The Luftwaffe General of Fighters, Adolf Galland, flew the recently delivered "V4" prototype on 22 May 1943. He enthusiastically endorsed the type and suggested that the Me-209 be cancelled. A few days later, the RLM placed an order for 100 production Me.262s.

Apparently even this decision did not clear away all the bureaucratic obstacles. Willi Messerschmitt kept on lobbying to produce both the Me-209 and the Me.262, partly it seems as an exercise in bureaucratic empire-building, and it wasn't until November 1943 that the Me-209 was dropped for good. Even then, the Me.262's political troubles were far from over, and in fact were just about to take a very nasty turn. Hitler, alarmed by the success of Allied amphibious landings in Africa and Italy, was very concerned about developing a fast fighter-bomber ("Jagdbomber / Jabo") to pin down invasion forces on the beaches until reinforcements could arrive to drive them back into the sea.

On 2 November 1943, Reichsmarshal Hermann Goering, head of the Luftwaffe, and Milch, visited the Messerschmitt plant in Augsburg. Goering asked Willi Messerschmitt if the new jet fighter could carry bombs. Messerschmitt answered without hesitation that the Me.262 had been designed from the outset to carry 500 kilograms (1,100 pounds) of bombs, could possibly carry twice as much, and would be easy to adapt to the "Jabo" role.

On 26 November 1943, Hitler inspected the Me.262 at Insterburg, and asked the same question: Can it carry bombs? Messerschmitt gave him the same answer that he had given Goering. Hitler's prayers had been answered. He ordered the Me.262 to be built as a fighter-bomber, and the Me.262 "Jabo" featured prominently in his military plans from then on. There is little record of anyone contesting his decision. The reality was that Messerschmitt completely ignored the will of the Fuehrer and busily worked to put the machine into production as a fighter.

Milch, on reading intelligence reports that the Americans were getting ready to field new bombers such as the Boeing B-29 that would be a handful for existing interceptors, also pressed on with production of the Me.262 as a fighter. Though Milch made agreeable noises about building it as a fighter-bomber, little or nothing was done to that end.

Me.262 into production

Whatever the political issues surrounding the Me.262 program, the real difficulty was that the aircraft was still a long way from being a production machine. At the time, there was only one Me.262 flying, the "V4" prototype. The previous three prototypes had been wrecked one way or another, and the "V5" prototype was being rebuilt to use tricycle landing gear, at the suggestion of Adolf Galland. Given the aircraft's long nose, the tail wheel landing gear configuration made forward visibility on the ground extremely poor, and the downward-pointing jets also tore up the runway.

The V5 had fixed nose gear, but was followed by the "V6" in October 1943, which had fully retractable landing gear and was close to production specification, and then the last test prototype, the "V7". By April 1943, 13 preproduction "Me.262A-0s" had been completed, of a total of 23 ultimately built out of the 45 ordered. These aircraft were close to production specification, but some had specialized test fits. For example, the "V12" was modified as a high-speed test article with a smaller canopy and other changes, and was clocked at 1,005 KPH (624 MPH), substantially faster than a standard Me.262.

Some of the preproduction machines were also sent on to the

Luftwaffe for operational evaluation by a group organised in April 1944 for the task, designated "Erprobungskommando (Proving Detachment) 262". It seemed like the Me.262 was coming into service at precisely the right of time, since now the US Army Air Forces (USAAF) had adequate numbers of long-range P-51 Mustang fighters to escort bombers on daylight raids over Germany, greatly complicating the air defence of the Reich. The Me.262 might well tilt the balance back to the defenders.

The problem was that building an adequate force of Me.262s was easier said than done. Messerschmitt was straining to keep up with demands for production of existing aircraft types, a difficulty that had been compounded by a devastating Allied air raid on the company's plant at Regensburg on 17 August 1943. Production had to be relocated to Oberammergau, near the Bavarian Alps. Delivering the temperamental Jumo-004 turbojets was even more troublesome.

Work muddled on into 1944, and then the political disconnect between the left and right hand finally led to an uproar. On 23 May 1944, Goering, Milch, Galland, other senior Luftwaffe officials, as well as Armaments Minister Albert Speer and his people, were called to Hitler's residence at Berchtesgaden to discuss the current fighter production program. The meeting was routine up to the point where production of the Me.262 as a fighter was discussed. Hitler was puzzled: "I thought the 262 was coming as a high-speed bomber. How many of the 262s already manufactured can carry bombs?"

Milch replied: "None, Mein Fuehrer. The Me.262 is being manufactured exclusively as a fighter aircraft." After a chilly silence, Milch then pointed out that the aircraft could not be adapted to the "Jabo" role without major design changes, and even then it would not be able to carry more than 500 kilograms (1,100 pounds) of bombs.

Hitler was shocked. Back in November, he had asked if the Me.262 could be adapted to the "Jabo" role, and was given an unqualified YES. He had ordered that it should therefore be built as a fighter-bomber, and nobody had protested the decision. He had been including the "Jabo" Me.262 in his plans for the defence of the Reich against an amphibious landing by the Western Allies, which was expected any time soon and in fact would take place within weeks, on 6 June 1944. Now Hitler was being told that not only were there no "Jabo" Me.262s, but that the assurances he had been given about its feasibility were false, and to make matters worse nobody had told him of any of this. That would have angered far milder men than Hitler, and he was furious: "Who pays the slightest attention to the orders I give? Hitler left nobody in any doubt that the aircraft was to be equipped as a fighter-bomber!"

Goering made excuses and passed the blame onto Milch, who was soon stripped of most of his powers. Hitler ordered that work now be focused on delivering the "Jabo" version of the Me.262, though he did consent to continue testing of the fighter version as long as it didn't slow down deliveries of the "Jabo" variant. Messerschmitt engineers now belatedly began to fit the "V10" prototype as a fighter-bomber that could carry two 250-kilogram (550 pound) bombs. The result was clearly an improvisation, but since the Arado Company was already working on an optimized jet bomber, the "Ar-234", the "Jabo" variant of the Me.262 could serve as an interim solution.

By late June 1944, a fighter-bomber unit, "Erprobungskommando Schenk", had been formed under Major Wolfgang Schenk. A month later, the unit was relocated to France with nine aircraft, in order to oppose the "real" invasion that was expected in the Pas de Calais, an expectation fostered by elaborate and comprehensive Allied deception programs.

The "Jabo" Me.262s in France accomplished little, and with the Allied breakout from Normandy they were gradually pulled back, to end up in Belgium at the end of August. With the invasion now history, Hitler rescinded the order to focus solely on the "Jabo" Me.262 version, and the focus of production returned to the fighter variant. The Fuehrer still insisted that any fighter variants that were built to be easily converted to the "Jabo" configuration on short notice.

Air raid defense remained in the foreground. 'Aviation' was the decisive keyword for 1944, and Hitler considered the fast bomber to be the most important factor entering the equation. Repeatedly Hitler asked how the Me.262 was coming along: he was impatient on the account of the long delivery date for the aircraft.

The Me.262 Displayed

Air raids on 22 and 23 November 1944 caused substantial devastation to the heart of Berlin. The Gauleiter of Berlin, Dr Groeb, reported personally to Hitler and made particular mention of the outstanding morale shown by the people of the city over the two nights. Hitler was again filled with rage and anger against the Luftwaffe, which was never able to stop a raid taking place. He repeated these criticisms in bitter terms on the 26 November at the impatiently awaited aircraft exhibition at Insterburg airfield. All those in some way responsible for aircraft production were present- Goreing, Milch, Speer, Saur, Messerschmitt, Galland, Vorwald and others. The Luftwaffe had repeated the error of setting out those models which were not ready for service. Hitler passed very calmly before the long line of aircraft, which included the newest version of the Me 109, Me 410, Ar 234, Do 335 and Me.262.

Milch accompanied him with full specifications to hand. Hitler was seeing the Me.262 for the first time was very impressed by the look of it. He called Messerschmitt over and asked him pointedly if the aircraft could be built as a bomber. The designer agreed, and said that it would be capable of carrying 250kg bombs. Hitler said "that is a very fast bomber" and gave the orders that Me.262 should be built exclusively as such.

Milch intervened at once to explain that only a number of the aircraft coming out off the production line could be released to the bomber role, but Hitler insisted.

Even Goering, when attempting to have Hitler's decision reversed a few days later, was rebuffed sharply.

As it turned out, however the Luftwaffe could only offer the type as a fighter-bomber because a true fast bomber would need extensive redesign for bomb carriage, release gear and sights. Hitler was forced to accept this.

Hitler often discussed Luftwaffe construction. Now he had decided to concentrate entirely on the production of fighters. These would have the highest priority. Everything else would be stopped. He expressed the hope daily that the first jets would soon be arriving in the front-line squadrons. However: the Me.262 could not be expected for at least another six months. But there was a great shortage of fuel, which Hitler himself didn't accept; some Army Group Centre units had reported severe shortages. Hitler said that what it amounted to was a struggle to protect the most important production centers and maintain the airworthiness of fighters. He acknowledged the fuel problems but said we must never give up the chance to obtain the upper hand. How we were supposed to do that without any fuel seemed to escape him.

Anger over the Me.262

At the daily situation conferences the enemy build-up for the channel invasion, and the resumption of operations in Russia and Italy, could be discerned as imminent. At the Centre-point of Hitler's considerations was the Me.262. In the end his desire to have it as a fighter-bomber failed owing to insurmountable technical difficulties, principally the alterations to the centre of gravity in the fuselage: a bomb-carrying capacity practically derived it of airworthiness. It was definitely completely unsuitable as a bomber. In a long talk at Obersalzberg on 23 May Goering explained all this to Hitler, who refused to accept the report. As far as possible he wanted 'all superfluous equipment' to be removed from the aircraft to make weight for at least one 250kg bomb. Milch, Galland, Peterson – the commanders of the Luftwaffe test centers- and others were unable to convince him that it would not work. Thus we simply had to wait until Hitler found out the hard way.

After further persuasions of the impracticality of his ideas, Hitler conceded that alternating the purpose of the Me.262 from fighter to bomber would create technical problems, but these had to be taken into account.

Hitler regretted only that the jet bomb design had not been contracted for earlier.

These conversations about the Luftwaffe led to a decision at the end of may that the entire responsibility for Luftwaffe production should come under the umbrella of Speer's ministry. The transfer was made in early June, after which Milch was relieved of his duties and retired to his hunting lodge north of Berlin.

He was in the picture as no other about the Luftwaffe production problems and knew that the air force was not adequate for the demands to be made on it in the near future.

Me.262 Schwalbe/Sturmvogel

The production "Me.262A-1a Schwalbe (Swallow)" fighter that finally emerged was fitted with two Jumo-004B engines with 8.83 kN (900 kgp / 1,980 lbf) thrust each. The "B"-series engines were production standard, using much smaller amounts of "strategic metals" such as chromium, nickel, and molybdenum than the pre-production "A" series engines. That made the "B" series engines substantially lighter than the "A" engines, but at a price, as described below.

The Jumo-004's starter system was unusual and worth

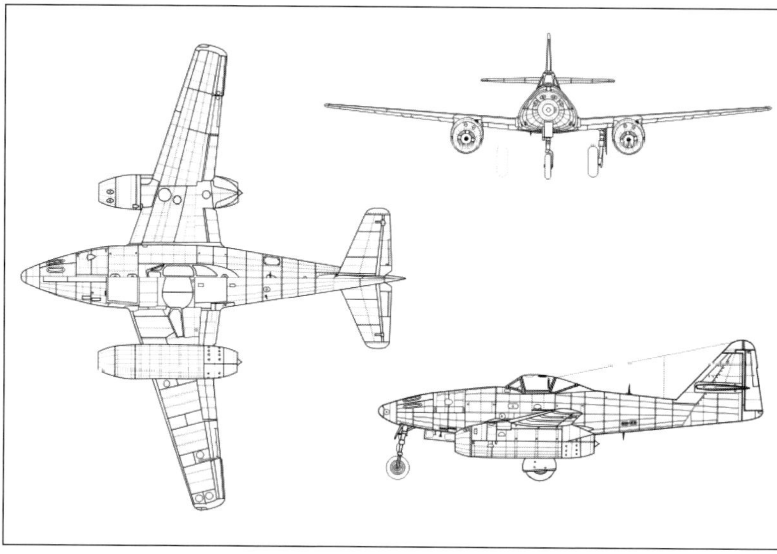

The Me.262 Schwalbe

comment. The compressor of a turbojet has to be brought up to speed before the turbojet can be ignited. In modern aircraft, this is done by a high-torque electric motor or airflow from a small starter turbine engine, while in many earlier jet aircraft it was done using a pyrotechnic cartridge that kicked the turbine into motion. The Jumo-004's starter system consisted of a small two-stroke gasoline engine hidden behind the engine nozzle bullet. The gasoline engine had an electric starter, but as a backup there was a pull-cord starter with the handle in a recess in the front of the bullet. Apparently the BMW-003 had a similar scheme.

The Me.262A-1a was armed with four short-barrelled MK-108 30 mm cannon in the nose. The MK-108 was a low-velocity weapon, only a step above an automatic grenade launcher, and in fact its explosive shells were referred to as "mines". However, although they didn't have long range, they had terrific killing power. The top pair of cannon had 100 rounds per gun, while the lower pair had 80 rounds per gun. The aircraft was originally fitted with a Revi 16B reflector gunsight, though this was later replaced by the Askania EZ42 gyroscopic gunsight.

ME-262A-1A: Spec	Metric	Imperial
Wingspan	12.5 meters	40 feet 11 inches
Wing area	21.70 sq meters	233.58 sq feet
Length	10.58 meters	34 feet 9 inches
Height	3.83 meters	12 feet 7 inches
Empty weight	3,795 kilograms	8,380 pounds
Max loaded weight	6,390 kilograms	14,080 pounds
Maximum speed	870 kph	540 mph / 470 KT
Service ceiling	12,200 meters	40,000 feet
Range	1,050 kilometres	650 MI / 565

The Me.262A-1a had armoured front window glass and an armoured seat back. The wing had moderate sweepback, with trailing-edge flaps and leading-edge slats. The pilot sat high in an all-round vision canopy that tilted open to the right. The machine was not fitted with an ejection seat. The aircraft was designed to be easy to manufacture, and avoided the use of critical materials.

The "Jabo" Me.262 variant was designated the "Me.262A-2a Sturmvogel (Storm Bird)". As noted, it was fitted with two stores pylons under the forward fuselage for two 250 kilogram (550 pound) general-purpose or cluster bombs, and only had the upper pair of MK-108 30 millimeter cannon.

Cockpit armour was largely eliminated, and an extra fuel tank was fitted in the rear fuselage to increase range. This fuel tank had to be emptied first; otherwise the Sturmvogel became dangerously tail-heavy after dropping its bombs. If that sounds half-baked, it should be noted that a similar fix was made to the North American P-51D Mustang to give it "Berlin & back" range, with similar results. Work was also done on an odd scheme where the Sturmvogel was rigged to tow a large bomb fitted with a small wing, but the aircraft tended to "porpoise" while towing the bomb, with one aircraft losing control and lost, the pilot bailing out safely. Other nasty problems also cropped up and the idea was abandoned, with the final report stating the scheme had proven "hazardous and unsatisfactory".

Two seat Me.262s / End of the line

The high performance of the Me.262 made a tandem-seat operational conversion trainer version very desirable, and such an aircraft, the "Me.262B-1a", was introduced in the summer of 1944. The trainer of course had dual controls, with the second seat replacing one of the fuel tanks. Range was extended by fitting two 300 litre (80 US gallon) external tanks under the forward fuselage, about fifteen were built.

The trainer development led to the impressive "Me.262B-1a/U1" night fighter, featuring "FuG-218 Neptun" long-wave length radar and "Naxos" centimetric-radar-homing gear, operated by the back-seater. Armament was two MK-108 30 mm cannon and two MG-151 20 mm cannon. The well-known Hajo Hermann put the type through trials in October 1944. The Neptun "antler" antennas slowed the aircraft down, but it was still faster than the hated British Mosquito, which preyed on German night-fighters.

During the following winter, Kurt Welter, head of "Kommando Stamp", used Me.262A-1a day fighters for "Wilde Sau (Wild Boar)" night fighting, and in April the unit obtained

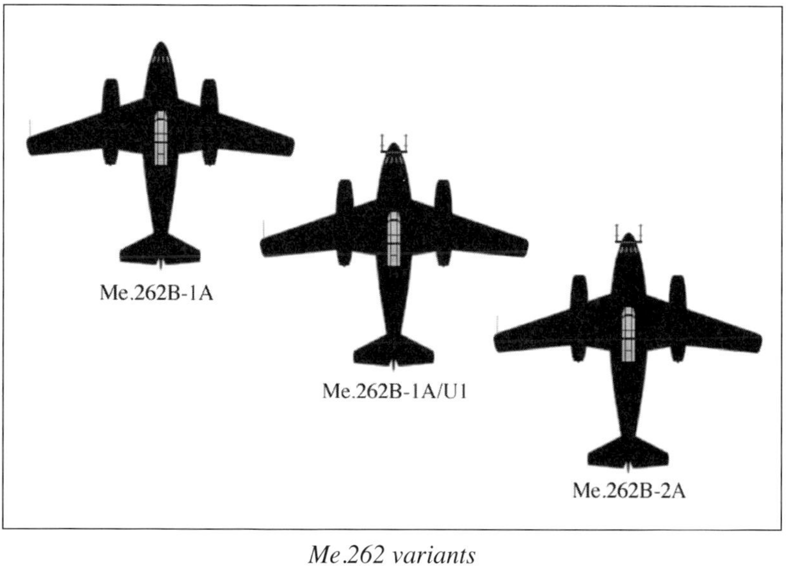

Me.262 variants

a few of the Me.262B-1a/U1 night-fighter variants. Despite all the difficulties, Welter claimed 20 kills, making him one of the first jet aces and likely the highest-scoring jet ace in all history.

By the end of the war, Messerschmitt was working on a prototype of the improved "Me.262B-2a" night fighter with a longer fuselage and increased fuel capacity. It was fitted with the Neptun radar at the outset, but there were plans to fit it with the "Berlin" centimetric radar, with improved range and resolutions and a dish hidden in the nose, instead of the clumsy and drag-inducing "antlers" of the long-wavelength radar. There was also consideration of fitting the Me.262B-2a with upward-firing cannon installed in the rear fuselage to allow it to attack RAF bombers from their belly blind spot.

However, as with all its sisters, the Me.262B-2a was too little and too late. The Jumo-004B engines were never very satisfactory for operational use. The fact that production engines had been designed to minimize use of precious high-strength metals meant that the blades tended to rapidly lengthen or "creep", and the engines sometimes had to be junked after as little as ten hours of flight operations.

Over 1,400 Me.262s were built, but only a relatively small portion of them ever saw action. Fuel was scarce, and Allied aircraft strafed and bombed at will. It appears that the Luftwaffe never had more than 200 on strength at any one time. The Me.262 shot down about 150 Allied aircraft, versus the loss of 100 Me.262s in action, an uninspiring war record.

The Me.262 had no real effect on the course of the war, though it would provide the Allies with plenty of inspiration in the post-war period. It was well in advance of anything the Allies had or had plans to build. Adolf Galland flew British Gloster Meteors in Argentina after the war and felt that if the Meteor's reliable engines had been mated to the Me.262's advanced airframe, the result would have been the most formidable of the first-generation jet fighters.

After the war, Me.262s that had fallen into Allied hands were evaluated by flight test groups, one of the best-known being a USAAF team named “Watson’s Whizzers”, led by Colonel Harold E. “Hal” Watson of USAAF Air Technical Intelligence. Watson’s pilots and ground crew managed to find intact Me.262s at the Lechfeld airstrip in Bavaria, and were assisted in their test flights by German ground crews familiar with the aircraft and even two English-speaking German test pilots, Ludwig Hofmann and Karl Baur. The Me.262s were then shipped to the US on the Royal Navy “jeep” carrier HMS REAPER for further evaluation at Wright Field in Ohio. The tests there included a competitive fly-off against a Lockheed P-80 Shooting Star jet fighter that concluded the Me.262 was generally superior.

A small number of Me.262s were completed or rebuilt in Czechoslovakia and flown by the Czech Air Force on an experimental basis. The Me.262A-1a became the “S-92”, while the Me.262B-1a trainer became the “CS-92”.

Minor variants and proposals

There were a number of interesting one-off variants of the Me.262.

A few of “Me.262A-1a/U1s” were built with two MK-108 low-velocity 30 millimeter cannon, two MK-103 high-velocity 30 millimeter cannon, and a pair of MG-151/20 20 millimeter cannon.

A number of “Me.262A-1/U2s” with instrumentation for all-weather operation were built as well. A ground-attack version, the “Me.262A-3a”, with additional armor and armament, was considered but not built.

A single “Me.262-2a/U1” Sturmvogel derivative was built with an experimental bombsight system. In addition, one or two “Me.262A-2a/U2s” Sturmvogel derivatives were built, with glass noses and a Lotfe 7H bombsight for a prone bombardier to permit horizontal bombing. Neither of these experiments

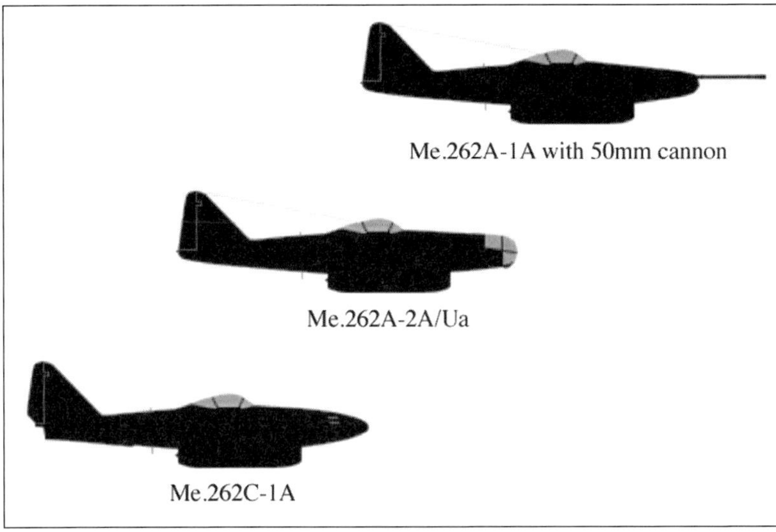

Me.262 variant designs

proved successful.

One Schwalbe was fitted with a Rheinmetall 50 mm cannon to shoot down Allied bombers. The big gun tended to jam badly, and it also seems that it blinded the pilot with its bright muzzle flash. The experiment was abandoned.

A number of reconnaissance variants were built, such as the "Me.262A-1a/U3" with no armament and the "Me.262A-5a" with two MK-108 30 millimeter cannon. They carried one or two nose-mounted cameras, and the Me.262A-5a could also carry two 300-liter external tanks. Some of these aircraft were flown in Italy just before the end of the war.

A single "Me.262C-1a" was built with a Walter booster rocket placed in the tail to improve climb for the interceptor role. A single "Me.262C-2b" was built with "BMW-003R" turbojet engines with built-in rocket boosters for the same purpose. It is said that this particular variant was tricky and frightening to fly.

Several other variants were considered but not built. The "Me.262 HG" featured wings with greater sweepback for high-speed performance and a "vee" or "butterfly" tail. Another scheme was a fairly sensible plan to build a bomber version with

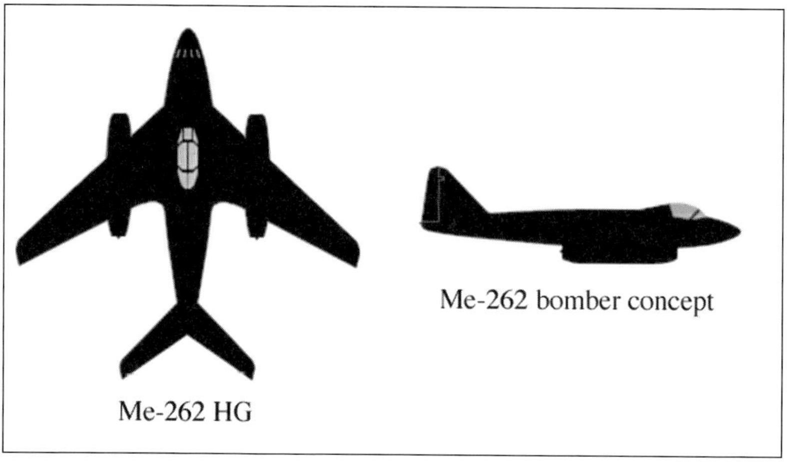

Me.262 bomber concept

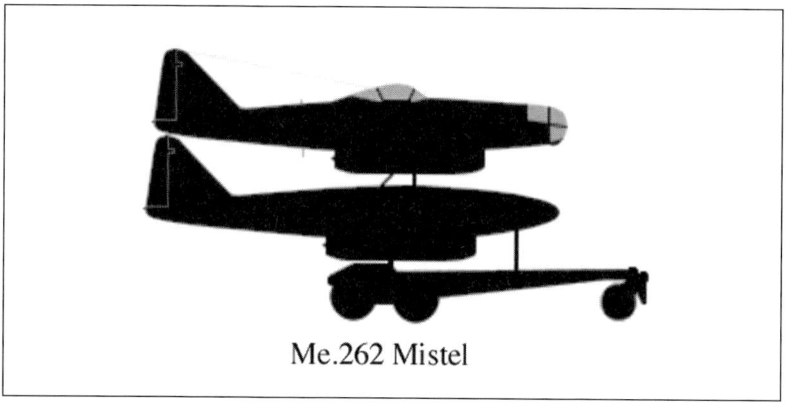

Me.262 Mistel design

an extended fuselage featuring a real bomb bay. This would eliminate the drag of the external bombs, increasing the speed of the aircraft and allowing it to outpace Allied fighters.

Since the long nose of the Me.262 led to poor pilot visibility, reconnaissance and bomber variants were proposed with the cockpit moved well forward, giving the aircraft something of the look of the Gloster Meteor. There was also a series of "Project 1099" two-seat heavy-fighter proposals which fitted the Me.262 wings and tail to a new, heftier fuselage, as well as a similar "Project 1100" bomber proposal — but these concepts were discarded since they were judged likely to be underpowered.

Ramjet and pulsejet boosted versions were envisioned, as well as a “Mistel (Mistletoe)” flying-bomb version of the Me.262 with no cockpit, a warhead in the nose, and a simple autopilot system. The flying bomb was to be controlled by a piloted Me.262 attached to a frame on top, with the whole clumsy assembly taking off on a big trolley that was dropped after take-off. The piloted Me.262 would release the flying bomb after pointing it at a target.

All of these concepts appear to have been nothing more than paper schemes, and it is doubtful that any of them got as far as mockups.

INTERROGATIONS AND DEBRIEFINGS

PLANS OF THE GERMAN FIGHTER FORCES FOR THE CONTINUATION OF WORLD WAR II

Interrogation Of Generalleutnant Galland at Kaufbeuren, Germany, 16-18 September 1945.

The following statements are not plans for a future war, but concern the projected developments for the fighter Force if the last war had not ended when it did. Most of the plans are discussed with reference to the air and ground situation as it existed at the beginning of 1945 before the Russians and Allies broke the Oder and Rhine lines respectively and it is presumed that Germany might have continued that war with the fronts on the ground much as they were at that time. As it actually did happen, the pushes from West and East made air war impossible for the Germans and resulted in the effective dissolution of the Luftwaffe by the end of April. This is how the Fighter Arm planned, at the outset of 1945, to continue defensive warfare in the air.

A. Technical Developments

(1) Conventional Fighters

Trends were towards high altitude fighters with long endurance. The Tank Ta-152C and 152H were in production and one Gruppe already had the Tank Ta-152 at the end of the war. These aircraft were to be powered with new high performance engines, the Jumo 213 and the Jumo 222. The Me.109H, a large Me.109 with a center section added to the wings for higher altitude performance and powered with the DB 603 or June 213, was cancelled late in 1944. Production of the F.W. 190 and Me.109 was to stop in 1945.

(2) Weapons for Conventional Fighters and Jets

The 30mm MK 103, with good ballistics up to 800 meters range, was to be introduced for use against bombers. It would replace the MK 108. The MG 213, either 2 or 3cm. was to be the standard fighter armament, replacing the MG 151 2 cm. The MG 213 had a cylic rate of fire of about 1000 rounds per minute and better ballistics than the MG 151 or MK 108. The R4M RP was eventually to replace cannon for use against bombers, possibly with a (proximity fuse) photoelectric cell device, which was almost perfected. The EZ 42 computing gyroscopic sight was to become standard equipment and a radar range measuring device for use with it was being developed.

(3) Accessories

For high altitude aircraft, special pressure cabins such as in the Tank Ta-152, cabin heating and de-icing, and high altitude parachutes (equipped with oxygen supply and with barometric pressure release) were planned and perfected. New types of external fuel tanks were not carried under the fuselage, but over the wing roots (flared in) or directly on top of the wings (flared in). It was found that the increased load of gasoline was most efficiently carried in these places.

(4) Radio

Navigation aids such as the Hermine were ready for use. By using simple click-stop tuning in various radio navigation stations, the map grid coordinates of the aircraft were shown on sliding scales in the aircraft, reducing navigational work to a minimum.

(5) Zerstörer (Heavy Fighters)

The Do.335 with three 30mm MK 103 cannon was planned as a fighter with ability to get away from the Allied fighter escort and at the same time to knock down bombers from a long range. It was also to be used at night against Mosquitos. The Do. 335 was in production when the war ended.

(6) Jet Aircraft

The Me. 262 was to be further developed to increase range, with drop tanks, better fuel, and a built-in Walther Rocket unit in the fuselage to increase climbing speed. More armament was to be built in and more armor was to be fitted for protection in attacking bomber formations. The He.162 Volksjager was not capable of much further development, except that it was to be improved until it came up to the first promises of Heinkel. Further developments would probably have resulted in the building of aircraft powered by both piston engine and jet units.

(7) Rocket Aircraft

The Me.163 with its short endurance and weak armament of 2 x MG 151 2cm., was to be replaced by the Me.263 with its doubled flying time and heavier armament of 4 x MG 151 or 2 x MK 108 (3cm.). A further armament for the Me. 263 was the use of two 5cm. rockets firing upward (or downward) from the forward wing roots, triggered by a photoelectric cell. The whole field of Flak rockets (like the Natter) was under the fighter arm. The pilots of these projectiles would be fighter trained, but the whole organizational set-up was still indefinite.

B. Planned Organizational Developments

(1) Conventional Fighters

With the fighter force fully on the defensive, Gruppen would have been held at a strength of about 70 aircraft, of which about 50 would be serviceable at anyone time. This was the maximum number which could start and assemble in a reasonable length of time. Big groups were also necessary so that the large fighter force could be fitted onto the small number of German operational airfields.

Operations would have been flown in Gruppe strength getting away from the big Gefechtsverbands of Geschwader size. Later, the Gruppen would fly in sight of each other. Eventually it was hoped to use R/T in the air for mutual support work between Gruppen. For once and for all, the old type of strict Division fighter control was to be done away with. Each Gruppe CO was to have tactical freedom about how and when he attacked the bombers. Mobility of fighter units would have been no longer necessary if the fronts had remained stable.

Fighters were to be specialized further into light and heavy Gruppen with appropriate armament for their respective duties of attacking the fighters and bombers. Since it was expected to use all units from time to time over the front in support of the Army, the heavy Gruppen were also to be trained to shoot rockets and drop bombs while the light Gruppen could strafe and fight off enemy fighters over the battle area.

The fear was that the Allied high altitude heavy bombers might begin to come in at a bombing altitude about 5000 feet higher than usual, which would have made all the German fighters very ineffective. This forced the introduction of the Tank Ta-152. It was planned to convert almost the whole conventional fighter force to this aircraft or the Me.1 09H for high altitude work. A small force of single engine night-fighters would have been kept in case German AI radar was completely jammed, in which case the SE fighters could have kept up some kind of a defense. Almost all twin-engine day fighter units had been dissolved and converted to SE fighters in early 1944, and it was planned to re-equip them with the Do.335s. Twin-engine fighters would still be used. They would be needed to satisfy the Navy's demand for cover for their U -Boats when approaching the continent.

C. Jet Aircraft Organization and Employment

(1) The use of the Me.262 and He.162 would have called for certain innovations in fighter organization and control. The Me.262 units utilized a Staffel of 12 aircraft, consisting of four

A captured Me.262 photographed around 1945

elements of three aircraft each. Gruppen were to have three Staffeln of 12 aircraft each, with four for the Gruppe Stab, a total of 40 aircraft. The 25 aircraft that would usually be serviceable would completely use up the average facilities of the German airfields available. Units were based on the Kette of three aircraft rather than on the Schwarm, consisting of four aircraft. Each Geschwader was to have three Gruppen because the Geschwader or the Gruppen were to provide their own fighter control and larger Geschwader would have been unwieldy. The employment of jets put great demands on fighter control. The great speed of jet aircraft made the time lag in reporting on the air situation of vital importance for fighter direction. Distance and direction estimations by formation leaders in the air were, for the same reason, often inaccurate. Jet fighters demanded very exact vectoring and information from the ground.

(2) The whole question of employment of the Me.262 was complicated by Hitler's order that it be used only as a bomber and by Goring's giving most of the aircraft to bomber units converted to fighter operations, assuming that the units could be ready for combat in time. Galland hoped to use the vastly

The Me.262 on an airfield circa 1945

superior Me.262 units against the Allied fighter escorts, which they could easily tie up by repeatedly diving and climbing to regain favorable position. Meantime the conventional German fighters could attack the bombers relatively unmolested, a job for which they were adequate from all standpoints, including armament, training, and aircraft performance. They had, by that time, little fear of the bombers' defensive fire.

(3) Actually the plan of using the Me.262's to attack the fighter escort never was put into effect, because by the time that the Me.262 fighter units O.G.7 in early 1945 and J.V.44 in April) were ready for operations, the conventional fighter force as such had ceased to exist. The Me.262s then had to attack the bombers because nothing else could. The Me.262's of J.G.7 and J.V.44 had considerable success even though they disregarded the Allied fighters. Whereas the former ratio of victories to losses had, with conventional fighters, been 1 to 5, with Me.262s it was reversed, one loss being suffered for every five victories.

(4) The use of the He.162 Volksjager presented very special problems. The aircraft was never satisfactory, though performance and safety equal to that of the Me.262 were

promised and probably would have been realized with further development. As it was, the aircraft went directly from the blueprint stage into final series production, without the usual testing and experimental stages. This was a marvelous feat of production, but the He.162 was not ready for combat at the end of the war. Its extremely short endurance, about 20 minutes, would have demanded it be directed in flight by a very skilled fighter control system. Combat missions would have to be timed so as to allow landings and takeoffs safe from the Allied fighter escort, which could easily destroy jets during landing and takeoff, when the jets could not accelerate or maneuver.

The He.162 units were to be employed as regional fighters to protect certain areas. The fighter control organizations concerned with them would probably have been their own Geschwader headquarters. They were set up similar to Me.262 Geschwader. One wild dream supported by Saur, the production wizard of the Jagerstab, was to use Me.262s and He.162s in the same formations, with the Me.262's leading. The Me.262s would have had the only R/T for command communications. The two dissimilar aircraft operating together would have been worth nothing.

Summary of debriefing German pilot Hans Fey on operational performance and late war deployment of the Me.262 jet fighter

Conducted by Major Ernst Englander, Spring 1945

THE MESSERSCHMITT 262

This report deals with the first Me.262 to fall intact into allied hands. Coupled with this good fortune is the happy circumstance that the pilot flew it into our lines deliberately and is knowledgeable and ready to impart his experience.

LAST FLIGHT

About 1345 hours on 30 March 1945, a strange aircraft with wheels down circled Rhein/Main airdrome. Occupying American troops on the field tried anxiously to identify it. The pilot carefully picked the only available field strip among the bomb craters, brought his ship in for a perfect landing, and stepped out of the cockpit.

He was Hans Fay, veteran Messerschmitt test pilot and technical inspector, with approximately 11,000 starts (80 in jet planes) to his credit. Fay had waited a long time for an opportunity which came as the result of two factors: first, the home town of his parents, near Lachenspeyerdorf, was at last in American hands, and second, 22 new jet planes which were in danger of capture at Schwabisch-Hall were ordered to be flown to Neuburg a/d Donau. When his family would no longer have to fear retaliation for his act, and when orders came on 30 March 1945 to proceed from Neuburg to Schwabisch-Hall to help ferry away the endangered jet planes, Fay saw his chance. He would fly his plane from Schwabisch-Hall to Lachen-Speyerdorf instead of Neuburg, turn it over to the Americans, and join his parents. Fay's account in this respect has been checked, and it is known that he informed his family of it last Christmas and again in

A rare photograph of an Me.262 crashed next to an autobahn

January. They in turn had told US authorities to be on the lookout.

Officials at the final assembly plant at Schwabisch-Hall had at first decided to destroy all jet planes on hand, since bombing had made the runways unusable. But at the last moment such repairs were completed as to justify a change of orders and an effort to ferry the planes out to safety.

Fay took off, fourth, and on gaining altitude, retracted his landing gear. But it was faulty, and failed to lock securely into place. For a moment Fay hesitated, then decided to go ahead with his plan. He flew on with landing wheels down at about 300 - 400 feet. His efforts to retract the landing gear brought him off course. Also, being slowed down considerably by the lowered landing gear, the pilot began to doubt his ability to reach Lachen-Speyerdorf. He quickly chose Rhein/Main as a substitute field, circled, picked a runway among the craters, and landed with a run of only 400/500 yards.

PERSONAL BACKGROUND AND MOTIVE OF INFORMANT

This pilot comes of an intellectual and artistic family which revealed anti-Nazi tendencies as early as 1935. They had barely managed to keep to themselves and avoid trouble with the Nazi regime. A younger brother was drafted early in the war, and was killed in the Polish campaign. A sister was drafted early in the war, into the service with a FLAK searchlight battery near Hannover, and managed simply to remain at home after leave in December 1944.

CAREER

Hans Fay was born in Speyer/Rhein in 1914. In 1932, after receiving the equivalent of a high school education, he entered on three years of aircraft construction and engineering training in Mannheim and Weimar. At the same time he received practical training as work student in tool factories and an auto repair shop

Fay got his basic (A/B) flying training in the Luftwaffe in

Darmstadt and Mannheim in 1936, then entered tactical training as a fighter pilot at Mannheim/Sandhofen in 1938. His main occupation during those years was office and construction work with Henschel Flugzeugbau in Berlin (1936), construction work with the firm of Prof. Max Meyer in Munich (1937), and the Allgemeine Elextrizitaets Gesellschaft (1937) in Berlin.

On 23 July 1939 informant was inducted into the Luftwaffe to participate in a flight teachers' course at Herzongenaurach, after which he was assigned to operational fighter units. In May 1940 he was transferred as test pilot to the Luftwaffe Erprobungsstelle (GAF Experimental Station) at Rechlin, where he tested the performance of captured enemy planes. During the winter of 1940/41 he was detached from Rechlin to Gardemoen, Norway, to make experiments with ski undercarriages on the Me 109 JU 87, and the Fieseler-Storch.

In August 1941 informant was discharged from the Luftwaffe, given professional deferment, and assigned from Rechlin as Me 109-acceptance pilot to the Erla Aircraft plants in Leipzig. From February 1941 to July 1942 he worked in the repair shops of Erla in Antwerp. There he also flew defensive missions, as test pilots at that time were called upon to do, and received the E.K. II (Iron Cross II Class) for shooting down a Spitfire. In August 1943 he returned to Erla-Leipzig, again as acceptance pilot for Me 109.

In September 1944 he was recalled into the Luftwaffe proper by Fliegersuber Kommando Quedlinburg and was returned to Erla on furlough status.

In December 1944, Fay was transferred by the German Air Ministry to Messerschmitt in Augsburg as acceptance pilot of the Me.262. On 1 January 1945 he started this new assignment with the Messerschmitt branch at Neuburg/Donau and Memmingen. He later continued this function in Neuburg until 1945 when he flew his aircraft to Rhein/Main.

THE Me.262 A-1 DESCRIPTION

German pilots called the Me.262 "Silber" ("Silver"). The particular ship flown by this pilot is established by papers which he brought along as series type A-1. He did not know of any other types except an ex- perimental Me.262. This was a two-seater with Plexiglas nose and no armament, which he saw at Lechfeld in January 1945. This plane was used for reconnaissance and possibly also for bombing.

All the general facts already known on the merits and demerits of the Me.262 in relation to the conventional fighter are confirmed by Fay. Its merits lie in its high speed and heavy armament, consisting of four MK 108 30mm cannons. Its demerits lie in its lack of maneuverability, its relatively short range, and in the extreme vulnerability of the jet units which tend to catch fire very readily if hit in aerial combat.

MARKINGS

Fay's aircraft had not been painted. The only markings on its silver skin were the conventional German black crosses on wings and fuselage, and the swastika on the fin. The customary paint for the operational Me.262 was a dark green camouflage spray, and a whitish spray for winter.

PROPULSION UNITS

The jet power plants were Jumo units designated "TL 109.004 B-1." The prefix "TL" probably stands for "Turbinelauf" (Turbine Movement). Both units were manufactured by the Junkers plant and were tested on the 5th and 14th of February, 1945.

ARMAMENT

The armament of this ship was normal, 4 x MK 108 30 Cm. cannon in the nose of the fuselage firing forward and synchronized for 500 yards.

GUN SIGHT

The gun sight is the old-fashioned REVI 16 B reflector-type which can be turned out of the pilot's field of vision. A fair number of the new Me.262's are now equipped with a gyroscopic sight.

ARMOR

The armor protection is a 16mm. bulkhead made in four sections at the forward end of the cockpit. Behind the pilot there is a 16mm. head and shoulder armor plate.

CANOPY

The canopy consists of two parts which can be jettisoned in one operation by pulling the red handle on the right hand side of the cockpit.

AUTOMATIC PILOT

Informant's plane had no automatic pilot. The first three Me.262's fitted with automatic pilots arrived in Neuburg toward the end of March 1945.

WEIGHT OF AIRCRAFT

A "Preliminary Flight Permission" (Vorlaeufige Fluggen Schimung) brought along by this pilot states that the maximum weight for starting is 710Q kgs (15,620 lbs). This includes the basic weight of the aircraft, 3870 kgs (8514 lbs) plus 3230 kgs (7106 lbs) allowance for fuel and bombs. If the weight when landing is more than 5700 kgs (12,540 lbs) special caution must be taken.

BOMB LOAD

There are two external bomb racks, but no internal bomb stowage. The maximum bomb load was stated by the pilot to be either 2 x 259 kgs (550 lb.) or 1 x 500 kg (1100 lb.) bomb. Lettering on the underside of the fuselage indicated the maximum carrying capacity at 500 kg. Based on the allowable weights, as shown by documents brought by the pilot, the indicated maximum bomb load might be 1000 kg (2200 lb.). Fay had never heard of such a load being carried.

FUEL TANKS

There are two main fuel tanks, one forward and one behind the cockpit, each with a capacity of 900 liters (238 U.S. gallons). Beneath the seat of the pilot is a reserve tank of 200 liters (53 U.S. gallons) capacity. Total fuel capacity is therefore close to 2000 liters (just over 529 U.S. gallons). The concentration of all tanks near the pilot makes his position extremely vulnerable.

FUEL

Fay knows of three varieties of fuel which can be used:

a. The standard fuel, used by him on all flights, a brown coal fuel oil known as J-2.
b. Diesel oil
c. Aviation gasoline.

Fay says that according to operating instructions, standard aviation gasoline was not considered so desirable because of its fast rate of consumption.

A small two-cycle starting engine uses gasoline mixed with 3"4% lubricating oil.

The brown coal fuel oil used at Neuburg came from an underground factory approximately 6 miles west of Neuburg near Unterhausen (Pinpoint of Unterhausen, 481190, GSGS4416, Germany, 1:1,000,000, sheet W 5 Augsburg). According to informant, this area was bombed, without success, toward the end of February 1945.

LENGTH OF RUNWAY

The length of runway required by an experienced pilot for takeoff and landing with the Me.262, with 1800 liters (475 U.S. gallons) fuel load and no bombs is estimated by informant as follows:

	CONCRETE	GRASS STRIP
Take-off	900 - 1100 yards	1100 - 1400 yards
Landing	900 - 1100 yards	700 - 900 yards

For an inexperienced pilot, Fay would add a safety margin of about 350 yards. When he landed at RHEIN/MAIN he was able, by excessive braking to bring the aircraft to a stop within

450-650.

For an additional tank load of about 200 liters (53 U.S. gallons) another 100 to 200 yards should be added to the above figures.

ASSISTED TAKE-OFF

Fay never used assisted take-off in his acceptance flights but he knows that such equipment is available for heavy loads or short runways.

PERFORMANCE ACCEPTANCE STANDARDS

In acceptance flights speed was the one requirement that was most strongly stressed. Test pilots and inspectors had orders to refuse delivery unless the aircraft meet the following specifications:

(a) Actual speed in straight and level flight at full throttle, 830 km/h (515 mph). Instructions were not to fly at this speed for more than 10-15 minutes, though informant believes that speed could be maintained for 20 minutes.

(b) Speed in a shallow dive, at about 30 degrees from horizontal, 950 km/h (589 mph). Speeds of from 1000 - 1050 km/h (620-650 mph) were spoken of as the absolute maximum for diving.

All planes tested by Fay met these speed specifications. He had heard of others which did not, but believes that after inspection and adjustments most aircraft finally met the speed requirements. However if the speed in level flight reached only 825 km/h (510 mph) or only 900 km/h (558 mph) in a dive, the ship was usually passed. That, however, was the extreme limit of tolerance.

Of a total of approximately fifty aircraft tested by informant, two were turned down. This was due not to failure to meet speed specifications, but to small structural defects on the plane as delivered or as the result of a slight bending of a wing of no more than 1 degree.

No more than ten percent of all aircraft tested were to be turned down and put aside for school machines. If the percentage of failure to meet operational performance specifications should be larger, the order was that the planes would have to be tuned and adjusted as much as possible and used for operations.

SPEED

Take-off speed with full fuel load but without bombs is about 180-200 km/h (111-124 mph). Cruising speed is about 750 km/h (465 mph).

In landing, the approach speed is 250 km/h (155 mph). Stalling speed with full fuel load is 180-200 km/h (112-125 mph).

In his entire acceptance flights Fay flew only up to 13,000 feet. Up to this altitude his experience was that the speed of the Me.262 does not change with changes in altitude, as is the case with ordinary aircraft. He attributes this primarily to the lack of a carburetor with its dependency on the density of the air, and the decreasing fuel injection pressure, more marked in jet units with increasing altitude than in the standard plane.

Fay believes that the speed of the Me.262 compares favorably with that of the AT 234, as the Arid is larger and heavier, and has the same propulsion units.

STRUCTURAL WORKMANSHIP

Fay says that the structural workmanship on the Me.262 is not as good as that on the Me 109. When testing the Me.262, it was not infrequent for parts to be stripped off in steep, fast dives, and Fay has himself lost cockpit covers, bomb racks, and the needle-valve of the tail-pipe during dives. In fact, because of these uncertainties, the pilots rarely did a roll or similar maneuver during acceptance flights.

RANGE

Flight duration of the Me.262 varies from 45 to 90 minutes. The maximum time of flight in low altitudes is 45 to 50 minutes; in

Me.262 B-1A/U1 night fighter (converted trainer), pictured on US testing ground after the war. Note the Neptun radar antenna on the nose and second seat for a radar operator.

high altitudes it ranges from 60 to 90 minutes. The reason for greater efficiency at higher altitudes lies in the dependency of the jet propulsion unit on the pressure of the air. The efficiency also varies with weather, namely barometric pressure and temperature. Fay says that the foreman in charge of jet propulsion units at Neuburg obtained daily data from the meteorological office on barometric pressure and temperature. Based on this information he made adjustments on the jet propulsion units to assure proper fuel pressure in order to obtain maximum efficiency in the consumption of fuel.

Range tables which are published by the Reichsluftfahrt-ministerium (German Air Ministry) for other aircraft types had not yet been made available on the Me.262 to the acceptance pilots. Fay believes therefore that range figures have not been finally established.

FLYING CHARACTERISTICS

Fay states that the Me.262 has good stall characteristics. The 262 has very good aileron control at all altitudes and at very high speeds, and it will do a good slow roll. He had never put one into a spin, but has stalled them intentionally. After stalling, it fell forward with no bad spin characteristics. As his -work as test pilot never took him above 13,000 feet, he has done no acrobatics other than slow rolls.

The 262 will turn much better at high than at low speeds, and due to its clean design, will keep its speed in tight turns much longer than the conventional type aircraft.

Spoilers (automatic slots) are fitted along the whole length of the leading cage of the wing. These come out automatically at about 300 km/h (186 mph) when the plane is in a glide angle and about 450 km/h (279 mph) when the plane is climbing.

There is no flutter while diving. Fay conjectures the reason for this to be the high position of the horizontal stabilizer in relation to the airflow around the wings.

About one third of the airplanes tested by Fay had a slight tendency to skid during their first flights. This has easily eliminated by adjusting the trim tab on the rudder.

SPECIAL PRECAUTIONS FOR JET AIRCRAFT

ACCELERATION

From 7000 to 8700 RPM, which is full power, the throttle may be increased quickly. Below 7000 RPM, the throttle must be increased smoothly and slowly.

A big error in the handling of the Me.262 is to increase the throttle too rapidly. Messerschmitt is therefore trying to develop a regulator that will automatically guarantee a smooth injection of fuel.

PARACHUTE

Informant believes that the parachute used by jet pilots is of a special type, as the ordinary type would tear when opened after bailing out at the great speed of the Me.262.

GROUND ACCIDENT WITH JET UNITS

A pilot who got too close to the jet units of a Me.262 was severely burned after walking about 3-5 feet in front of it and being pulled to the unit by the suction of the airflow. A safety minimum of at least 7 feet was prescribed in front and behind the jet units. Particular caution was to be exercised when starting, for occasionally the burning gasoline mixture ejects a flash flame from the rear of the jet unit.

VISIBILITY

With the exception of visibility, the minimum weather conditions for safe flying are the same for jet aircraft as for the conventional fighter. Because of its great speed, minimum safe visibility for take-off and landing of the Me.262 is considered at 4 - 5 K (2 1/2 to 3 miles) for a reasonably experienced pilot who knows the terrain. There were no blind-flying instruments in the aircraft, other than the artificial horizon.

CONVERSION TRAINING ON THE Me.262

Fay is acquainted only with conversion training at Neuburg. This base was particularly suitable because it has a concrete runway which is.2200 yards long. Therefore nearly all acceptance pilots in Ergänzungsgruppen (Training Units) of KG 40, KG 51, and KG 54.

Fay says that this aircraft is easier to fly than the latest types of FW 90 or Me 109- In fact, he feels any Me 109 pilot is qualified to fly the Me.262 after one hour's instruction.

Training consisted of ground instruction followed by three flights. The former bomber pilots flew a two seater Me.262 first and the regular Me.262 afterwards. During the first solo flight they were aided on the individual manual operation by W/T guidance from the ground. Only approximately 5% had any difficulties in retraining.

This training was followed by tactical training which included some formation flying and bombing practice.

After heavy bombardment of Neuburg in March 1945 the retrained bomber pilots were to be transferred to Munchen-Riem.

Retrained bomber pilots, while not as aggressive nor as effective in direct fighter attacks as experienced fighter pilots, are found to be quite satisfactory for the usual tactical use of the Me.262, which was to draw off our fighter cover, leaving the actual attack on our bombers to the Me 109's and FW 190's.

JET BASES AND PRODUCTION

Fay knows of the following airbases as final assembly fields for jet aircraft:

ESTIMATED NUMBER OF AIRCRAFT		
	Optimum Production (Monthly)	**Actual Production (Monthly)**
Kitzingen	40	20
Leipheim	180	50
Neuburg	120	80
Obertraueling	150	130
Schwabisch Hall	180	150
Total	**670**	**530**

OTHER BASES

Informant believes that Brandenburg/Briest was also used temporarily as one of the jet bases, and he has heard of Landsberg as a base for acceptance flights.

Accepted aircraft were ferried to operational jet units at Giebelstadt, Achmer, and one near Berlin, as well as other bases not known to informant. LOSSES Giebelstadt

Informant estimates that only approximately 50% of the entire Me.262 production is operational at any time. The losses occur in ferrying, conversion training, and as a result of occasional failures of the jet propulsion units. Frequent air alerts and raids delay and reduce the production. Bombardment of component plants caused stoppages in supply of spare parts. Considerable difficulty was experienced in getting jet units from Muldenstein, and they often had to wait for days to get sufficient gasoline to send a truck to Muldenstein.

ALLIED AIR ATTACKS ACTION IN CASE OF AIR RAID ALARM AT NEUBURG

The airfield received its first warning when Allied aircraft were reported within a 150 km (93 miles) radius. They then instructed

Flying Control that no aircraft were to take off and that any of their aircraft on test flights in the vicinity were to land and be parked in dispersal areas and revetments. Aircraft in the air were instructed over FuGe 16 "Machen Sie sofort Lucy Anton," code for "land at once," too far away from their own base were told over FuGe 16 "Machen Sie sofort Lucy Anton, i.e. Kitzingen", code for land at once at Kitzingen, or any other suitable base which was not likely to be under attack at the same time. The rest of the message was in open language and sometimes even added "enemy fighters" or "enemy bombers" or "enemy jabos" (fighter bombers) in the vicinity. Fay said they ordered their 262's to land, as they would not have enough fuel left to engage in combat after an acceptance flight.

On the second warning, Allied aircraft were supposedly within about 100 km (62 miles) and all personnel were to leave the immediate vicinity. They would go in autos to about 10 km distance, or on bicycles or on foot as far as they could go.

RAID ON NEUBURG

The raid on Neuburg at the end of March 1945 destroyed almost all ground equipment and installations and most tools and spare jet units. All aircraft on the field, that is, an approximate total of 80-100 Me.262 were destroyed or damaged on the ground. This included about 60 aircraft of the Ergänzungsgruppen (retraining units), about 20 of the "Moorkultur" (code name for the acceptance unit) and about 20 of the final assembly " Wandmontage " at Zell.

The runway was usable again after three days. If the craters are small, repair usually takes only one to two days. Informant said that fragmentation bombs were particularly effective against the dispersal positions, but H.E. bombs were more effective in destroying the aircraft in hangars and in damaging runways.

Informant though that bombing of Neuburg runways, hangars and dispersal areas was more effective than bombing of living quarters.

This was the first Me.262 to come into Allied hands when its test pilot defected in March 1945. It was subsequently lost in August 1946, the US test pilot parachuting to safety.

Jets were usually tested right in front of hangars. In case of alert they usually dispersed the Me.262's quickly. At Memmingen only it was the customary procedure to pull the jet planes into hangars.

RAID ON OBERTRAUBLING

Fay heard from a reliable source that in the Obertraubling raid about the end of February or beginning of March 1945, approximately sixty Me.262's were destroyed. This raid was particularly effective, as this field had no concrete runway and the ground was so soft that the Me.262's could not take off when the alert was sounded.

RAID ON LEIPHEIM

Fay heard that in this raid toward the end of March 1945, thirty Me.262's were destroyed.

AUTOBAHN STRIPS FOR JET AIRCRAFT

As jet airfields available to the GAF become fewer, a policy is coming into effect of using camouflaged sections of superhighways (Autobahn) for landing strips, and of using the adjacent woods as dispersal areas. The ground crews and pilots of the Fuehrerkurierstaffel under Hptm. Talk were stationed in Neuburg until the air raids at the end of March 1945. It was planned that this staffel would use the stretch or the Autobahn between Muenchen and Augsburg at Lechhausen as a landing strip (Pinpoint: from 357840 - 383834, GSGS 4416, Germany 1:100,000, sheet W 5, Augsburg). Work on this particular airstrip was begun a few months ago, but could not be finished due to lack of transportation facilities and building materials. In March 1945 Hptm. Talk wanted to finish it quickly, with the help of a GAF Construction Battalion (Luftwaffen-baubataillon).

Other such landing strips were to be built and may now be under construction at the following pinpoints: 861843 to 890847, Germany, 1:100,000, GSGS 4416, sheet W 4, ULM and somewhere between 736200 and 740310, Germany 1:100,000, GSGS 4416, Sheet V 6, Regensburg. On these Autobahn airstrips the grass in the middle of the road is removed and the ground covered with asphalt and then camouflaged to give it its original appearance. Any overhead obstructions such as bridges of intersecting highways are dynamited to give a line of approach without obstacles. In the opinion of informant, it should be easy to observe the construction of these landing strips from the air before they are camouflaged.

COUNTERTACTICS SUGGESTED FOR ALLIED FIGHTERS AND BOMBERS

The GAF has apparently not yet perfected the best tactics with the jet plane. Fay heard from another pilot and some crew chiefs that several Staffeln of Me.262's at Lechfield devoted themselves primarily to flying experimental missions against Allied aircraft to devise the best method of attack.

Informant made the following suggestions on combating the Me.262. These are theories, as he has no combat experience with jet aircraft. Although some of these suggestions are obvious, they are presented because they confirm tactics used in the past by Allied pilots.

(1) Aim at the jet propulsion units, as they catch fire even more easily than the conventional engine.

(2) Overcome the advance in speed by an advantage in altitude. By flying the fighter cover in a stacked-up formation with as much as 3,000 feet between flights, the high flight could reach a speed in dive similar to that of the Me.262, and exploit this in attacking. Furthermore, the Me.262 is relatively slow in turns and movements. It cannot, for instance, Split-S in less than 9000-12000 feet. The ideal situation would be a combination of two factors: first, speed gained through superior altitude, thereby making straight escape risky to the jet aircraft, and second, exploiting its lesser maneuverability when it goes through an evasive maneuver.

(3) Catch the Me.262 in its traffic pattern. It is particularly vulnerable when landing, as it is then likely to be low on fuel.

Fay tells of an incident which happened about six weeks ago when two P-51's were reported in the Memmingen area, then proceeded at minimum altitude below radar cover. and suddenly reappeared at the Neuburg A/D. They exploited this surprise element by shooting down a Me.262 while in the process of landing.

Cannons of the Me.262 are adjusted for the fire to converge at 450 meters (500 yards). Therefore, when it attacks a bomber formation, it is imperative that the bombers shoot a strong field of fire from a relatively long range before the jet aircraft has an opportunity to use its devastating fire-power.

PERSONALITIES

Fay does not give the impression of being an opportunist, and seems to regret only that the Americans did not capture his hometown earlier so that he could have brought his plane and himself to the Allies even sooner. He expects a very early collapse of German resistance, and is willing to help the Allied war effort in any practicable way, in order to avert further

Name	Location	Function
Stabsing. Bader	Rechlin	Experimental station test pilot, works on new types of aircraft.
Ing. Beauvais	Rechlin	Experimental station test pilot, works on new types of aircraft.
Hptm. Bender	Neuburg	KG. 54
Braendle (Brendle)	Obertraubling	Chief Pilot for Messerschmitt plant.
Hpt. Ing. Brueckner	Location not known	RLM Supervisor Chief of all German Aircraft Production.
O'Stabsing. Franke	Location not known	Director at Heinkel formerly in Rechlin, he was promoted from Gefreiter to Leutnant for having sunk the Ark Royal.
Hoffmann (not a Nazi)	Neuburg	Control pilot of RLM also at Memmingen and Leipheim airfields.
Kaden	Neuburg	Chief Jet Pilot and "Flugbetriebsleiter" for series production of Messerschmitt.
Oblt Kersting (Not a Nazi)	Neuburg	Specialist at Junkers Motors on turbines, and test pilot at Messerschmitt.
Dipl. Ing. Koch	Memmingen	Dir. Linder Regensburg Chief at Messerschmitt Works for series production of Me 262.
Prof. Lippich	Location not known	Aircraft Engineer and specialist in aerodynamics.
Shlinz	Neuburg	Supervisor of acceptance flight department.
Hptm. Talk	Lechhausen	Chief of "Fuehrerkuriestaffel" Lechhausen near Augsburg.
Hptm. Thieme	Neuburg	KG. 54
Meister Waggenhut	Memmingen	Foreman
Ing. Witt	Schwabisch Hall	Supervisor of Assembly plant.

unnecessary bloodshed, and to get the Nazis off the neck of the German people.

He is prepared to fly his ship for test purposes or in mock combat with our own jet and other fighter planes. His character and general reliability have been checked. The interrogation officer also visited his family. It is felt that Fay acted in good faith, without ulterior motives, and with the courage of his convictions. He is regarded as trustworthy.

Ernst Englander, Major, Ac.
For Eric M. Warburg, Lt. Col., Ac.

TOP SECRET - Interrogation of Reich Marshal Hermann Goering

(Because General Patch is personally responsible for the safe custody of the prisoner, it is necessary for General Spaatz' party to go from Headquarters Ninth Air Force to Headquarters Seventh U.S. Army).

Reich Marshall Goering was standing in a small office of the school wearing grayish wool, no medals but epaulets of a Field Marshal; (that is, a large eagle, a small Swastika, and crossed batons.) He had a silver ring on the third finger of his right hand. Blue eyes, ruddy not unpleasant face, big thighs, tan boots.

Interpreter provided by the Seventh Army.

Those present were:

- Reich Marshall Herman Goering.
- General Spaatz. CG, USSTAF.
- Lt. Gen. Patch (part of the time) CG, 7th Army.
- Lt. Gen. Vandenberg, CG, Ninth Air Force.
- Brig. Gen. E.P. Curtis, C/S USSTAF.
- Brig. Gen. Paul Barcus.
- Major Alexander de Seversky, Special Consultant to Secretary of Far.
- Dr. Bruce Hopper, Historian, USSTAF.

SPAATZ: Would you tell us something the organisation of the Luftwaffe and the plans, especially the factors that went into the non-fulfillment of those plans?

GOERING: In the early years when I had supreme command of the Luftwaffe. I had definite plans, but in 1940 Hitler began to interfere, taking air fleets away from our planned operations. That was the beginning of the breakdown of the Luftwaffe efficiency.

SPAATZ: In the battle of Britain why did you maintain such rigid formation of fighters and bombers?

GOERING: It was necessary to cover the bombers because there fore power was low (not like your bombers). It was also necessary for our fighters to closely cover each other. You see, it was a question of equipment.

SPAATZ: Was the JU 88 designed for the Battle of Britain?

GOERING: The JU 88 was primarily a commercial airplane that had to be adapted for the Battle of Britain along with the HE 111 because we had nothing else. I was not in favour of engaging in the Battle of Britain at that time. It was too early. The HE 177 was in late development. The HE 177 was development from the original Stuka with two propellers on four motors. It was a failure; it wasted two years. That is why we had no large bombers in the Battle of Britain.

SPAATZ: When did you know that the future of Luftwaffe was loosing control of the air?

GOERING: When the American long-range fighters were able to escort the bombers as far as Hanover, and it was not long until they got to Berlin.

We then knew we must develop the jet planes. Our plans for the early development of the jet was unsuccessful only because of your bombing attacks.

SPAATZ: Did our attacks affect your training program?

GOERING: Yes, for instance the attacks on oil retarded our the training because our new pilots could not get sufficient training before they were put into the air, where they were no match for your flyers.

PATCH: Did the Luftwaffe have priority in the distribution manpower?

GOERING: Yes the Luftwaffe had first priority and thus has the dream of Germany, the U-Boats were second, and the Panzers third. Even at the end the best German Youth went into Luftwaffe. Only the Waffen SS sometimes held back personal. All the other organisations surrendered personnel to the Luftwaffe on application.

The Me.262 Night Fighter

SPAATZ: Did the jet airplane really have a chance to win against us?

GOERING: Yes, I am still convinced, if we had only four to five months more time. Our underground installations were practically all ready. The factory at Karla had a capacity of 1000 to 1200 jet airplanes a month.

Now with 5000 to 6000 jets the outcome would have been different.

VANDENBERG: But could you train sufficient jet pilots, considering your shorts of oil?

GOERING: No, because German industry was going underground, and our counter measures could have kept pace with your bombing. But the point is that if Germany were attacked in her weakened condition as now. Then the air could do it alone. That is, the land invasion meant that so many workers had to be withdrawn from factories' production and even from Luftwaffe.

PATCH: Was that also true of England?

GOERING: To me, that is a different question. Germany was prepared for war and England wasn't. I was forced by Hitler to divert air forces to the east (which I always opposed). Only the diversion of the Luftwaffe to the Russian front saved England. She was unable to save herself and unable to bomb Germany.

SPAATZ: When you conquered France in the 1940, why didn't you go on through to Spain and Gibraltar?

GOERING: Germany had saved Spain from Bolsheviks. Spain was in the German camp. I insisted on going to Spain but to no avail. We could have bottled to British Fleet in the Mediterranean, but no, the Fuehrer wanted to go to Russia. My idea was to close both ends of the Mediterranean, "Und dann die sache 1st in ordnung." I am positive we could have taken Gibraltar. The Luftwaffe was ready and we had two divisions of parachutists ready and trained, but Mussolini objected. Part of our pain - the Italians. Also there was the complication of the relations between France and Spain.

SPAATZ: Did you know anything of our movement to Africa as to time and place?

GOERING: Well, I presumed it, but if the Germans had only held Morocco and the Canneries as I wanted, the going would have been different for you.

SPAATZ: Your best attack on us was at Poltava, at the airfield. Why was that so successful?

GOERING: Those were wonderful times. We had an observation ship flying with you. You did not know it. It was a 177 which fortunately developed motor trouble and indicated it couldn't land on the field with only one motor. So it was unable to return to give the information on your landing at Poltava. As we had an attack planned on a railway nearby we merely diverted it to your airfield.

VANDENBERG: Will you tell me why you bombed cities in England instead of concentrating on aircraft and engine factories?

GOERING: My intention at first was to attack only military targets and factories, but after the British attacked Hamburg the

people were angry and I was ordered to attach indiscriminately.
SPAATZ: Which had the more effect in the defeat in Germany, the area bombing or the precision bombing?
GOERING: The precision bombing, because it was decisive. Destroyed cities could be evacuated but destroyed industry was difficult to replace.
SPAATZ: Did the Germans realise that the American Air forces by intention did only precision bombing?
GOERING: Yes. I planned to do only precision bombing myself at the beginning. I wanted to build a wall of contact mines around Britain and close the ports but again I was forced to do otherwise by political Diktat.
CURTIS: Was our selection of targets good, particularly oil?
GOERING: Yes, excellent. As soon as we started to repair an oil installation you always bombed it again before we could produce one ton.
VANDENBERG: Why didn't you attempt to cut us off in Africa and send the Luftwaffe, which was superior in the air, against our shipping and the concentration of our airplanes at Gibraltar?
GOERING: We had too few/long-range airplanes and then, later, when you got to Algiers the airfields in Italy were inadequate. You have no idea what a time we had in Italy. If they had only been our enemies instead of our allies we might have won the war.
SPAATZ: Why did you use your bombers to haul gas to Rommel instead of bombing the line of communication from Algiers to Constantine to Tunisia?
GOERING: Higher HQ orders.
VANDENBERG: Why did you attack our airdromes on 1 January 1945?
GOERING: Because every airdrome was loaded with airplanes.
VANDENBERG: Well, why didn't you come back?
GOERING: Orders from higher headquarters. Hitler said it was no good to bomb American planes because more of them would

come like bees.

VANDENBERG: But why did you concentrate on RAF airfields more than on ours?

GOERING: Because the RAF airfields were closer and otherwise more inviting targets. We used 2300 planes for the attack; what we did not allow for was the intense concentration on AA guns placed there against the V-1.

VANDENBERG: Would you contrast the Air Forces of the Allies?

GOERING: Well the Russians are no good, except on undefended targets. You need only three or four Luftwaffe airplanes to drive off a twenty-plane Russian attack.

The Americans are superior technically and in production. As for the personnel, the English, German and American are equal as fighters in the Air.

SPAATZ: Have you any knowledge of a proximity fuse?

GOERING: Yes, in three or four months there would have been production.

SPAATZ: Has Japan the designs of this fuse?

GOERING: I do not think so because it was not yet in production and we never gave them anything unless it was in production. The Japanese have had the designs of the Me.262 for some time.

Goering then talked for several minutes, the gist of which emphasised our successful use of radar and counter-radar measures, to which he attributes much of the success of our operations.

SPAATZ: If you had to design the Luftwaffe again, what would be the first airplane you would develop?

GOERING: The jet fighter and then the jet bomber. The problem of speed has been solved. It is now a question of fuel. The jet fighter takes too much. The jet bomber, ME 264, designed to go to America and back, awaited only the final solution of the fuel consumption problem. I might add that

Underground military production of the Me.262 in the REIMAHG works.

according to my view of future airplanes is one without fuselage (flying wing) equipped with turbines in combination with the jet and propeller.

SEVENSKY: In view of your diminishing manufacturing recourses, who made the decision to divert a large portion of your national effort to manufacture of V-1 and V-2 weapons instead of building up the Luftwaffe?

GOERING: Well, there was great confusion of thought in Germany, Prior to the invasion the V-1 would have been effective. After the invasion our effort should have been concentrated on the Me.262 (jet). The decision on the V-2 project was made at higher headquarters.

VANDENBERG: In the tactical operations of our Air force, what attacks on what targets were most damaging to you?

GOERING: Before D-Day it was the attacks on Northern France which hurt the most because we were not able to rebuild in France as quickly as in Germany. The attacks on Marshalling yards were most effective, next came the low-level attacks on troops, and then the attacks on bridges. The low flying airplanes

had a terror effect and caused great damage to our communications. Also demoralizing were the umbrella fighters, which after escorting the bombers would swoop down and hit everything, including the jet planes in process of landing.

SPAATZ: Did you have a three-inch gun for the jet?

GOERING: The 5.5 centimeter machine gun, only now going into production would have made a great difference in the jet. While waiting for that we used the 5.5-centimeter rocket. You might find around Germany some more airplanes equipped with anti- tank guns. Don't blame me for such monstrosities. This was done on the explicit orders of the Fuehrer. Hitler knew nothing about the air. He may have known something about the Army or Navy, but absolutely nothing about the air. He even considered the Me.262 to be a bomber; and he insisted it should be called a bomber.

SEVENSKY: I know that four-engine Focke-Wulf planes were in production in 1939. When you found after the Battle of Britain that your planes did not have sufficient fire power and bombing power, why didn't you concentrate on their four-engined planes as a heavy bomber?

GOERING: Instead of that, we were developing the HE 177 and tried to develop the Me.262, which was designed to go to American and return. We did use the Focke-Wulf against shipping in Norway. Because our production capacity was not as great as that off America we could not produce quickly everything we needed. Moreover, our plants were subject to constant bombing so that it was difficult to carry out our plans for heavy bomber production.

SEVENSKY: The reason why I asked the previous question was because I wanted to establish whether you failed to build the big bombers because you did not believe in strategic air power or because your productivity capacity was restricted to the production of tactical aircraft for the Russian Campaign.

GOERING: No, I always believed in strategic use of air power. I built the Luftwaffe as the finest bomber fleet, only to see it wasted on Stalingrad. My beautiful bomber fleet was used up in transporting munitions and supplies to the army of 200,00 at Stalingrad. I always was against the Russian Campaign.

ME.262 A-1 PILOTS HANDBOOK

BY F.D. VAN WART, 1ST LT., AIR CORPS.
DATE PREPARED: 10 JANUARY 1946.
RELEASE DATE: 15 JULY 1946

Section 1 - DESCRIPTION

GENERAL

a. The Me.262 is a single-place, jet-propelled aircraft used as a fighter-bomber. The low swept-back wing is a symmetrical airfoil section with square tips. Automatic leading edge wing slots are incorporated in the wing design. The fuselage of the Me.262 is triangle shaped with an unusually long nose, and a tail assembly of a single fin and rudder. The under- carriage is a squat tricycle type. Two propulsion units under the wing provide power.

b. The approximate dimensions of the aircraft areas follows:
(1) Wing span 41 ft.
(2) Overall length 34 ft. 9 in
(3) Height of fin above the ground 11 ft. 4 in.

c. The airplane gross weight runs between 10,154 lb. (empty) and 14,272 lb. (with maximum fuel).

d. The propulsion units consist of two Junkers TL (Jumo 004) axial- flow type jet engines. The power output is controlled by the rate at which fuel is supplied to the burners.

FLIGHT CONTROLS

a. The flight controls are conventional, using push-pull rods throughout.
(1) The ailerons were designed to use servotabs, but the aircraft received have had the aileron tabs converted to a ground adjustable type, using turnbuckles for adjustment.
(2) The elevator trim tabs were also intended to be of the

servotype, but on the aircraft received, have been fixed by riveting in position.

(3) The rudder employs a controllable tab, operative from the cockpit. The tab control is on the left side of the cockpit. A position indicator indicates the amount of tab adjustment.

b. There is a horizontal stabilizer trim control and indicator. The angle of incidence of the stabilizer is varied by an electric motor to trim the aircraft. Control is operated by lever. Horizontal stabilizer position is shown on indicator. Power is supplied to the controls by the switch in the main switch panel.

c. Wing flaps.

(1) The Handley-Page type flaps are operated by two push buttons. Flap position is indicated by graduations of 0°, 10% 20°, 30°, 40% and 50° marked on the upper surface of the flap; the 20° position used for take-off is marked in red.

(2) Emergency lowering of the wing flaps is accomplished by the use of an emergency compressed air system. Operation is accomplished by opening the operating handle two complete turns.

Warning: Be sure the valve is opened two complete turns.

THROTTLE CONTROLS

The throttle controls are located at the pilot's left, and are the only power controls on the airplane. The black buttons, one on each throttle, are used to close the circuits for starting ignition on the engines. The throttles are equipped with stops to prevent accidental full closing and stalling of the engines.

LANDING GEAR CONTROLS

a. Under normal conditions the landing gear is raised or lowered by use of the two push buttons. It is hydraulically operated, but because of the low capacity of the hydraulic pump, it is slow in operation.

b. Compressed air is used for emergency operation of the under carriage, but lowers the nose wheel and main undercarriage fairing only. The undercarriage itself falls under the influence of gravity, and locking may require the assistance of slide slipping. Operation of the compressed air emergency system is accomplished by opening the operating handle at least two complete turns.

Warning: Be sure to open two complete turns.

c. Landing gear position indicators are provided for each unit of the undercarriage indicator, left main gear indicator, nose wheel, and indicator, right main gear.

BRAKE CONTROLS

a. The brakes embody a conventional hydraulic system, independent of the landing gear and flap hydraulic system. Operation is accomplished by applying pressure with the toes on the rudder pedals.

b. A brake is also incorporated in the nose wheel. Operation is accomplished by use of the nose wheel brake control lever.

HYDRAULIC SYSTEM CONTROLS

a. The engine driven hydraulic pump is in operation whenever the port engine, to which it is attached, is operating. Because of the low capacity of the pump, operation of the landing gear is slow, and time allowance must be considered when approaching for a landing.

b. Hydraulic power is used to operate the flaps and landing gear.

c. A compressed air emergency system is incorporated to be used for lowering flaps and landing gear in event of failure of the hydraulic system.

ELECTRIC CONTROLS

a. The electrical system is in operation whenever the battery switch, and the generator switches, are in the "on position".

b. A circuit breaker is located to the left side of the cockpit, and relieves the entire electrical system in the event of an overload. The circuit breaker can be reset by pushing the button.

c. The external power supply plugs into a socket on the right hand side of the fuselage just above the wing.
d. The inverter switch is located in the main switch panel.

FUEL SYSTEM CONTROLS

a. The capacities of the four (4) fuel tanks areas listed:

1. Front main fuel tank ....240gal.
2. Rear main fuel tank ....204gal.
3. Front auxiliary tank ....53gal.
4. Rear auxiliary tank ....158gal.

Total ....655 gal.

b. Fuel is supplied to the engines from the two main fuel tanks, one located in front of the pilot and one in back of the pilot. Either engine can be supplied from either tank, depending upon the position of the fuel selector and shut off controls located next to the throttles. The fuel pumps are put into operation by the push button switches located in the main switch panel.
c. Fuel transfer is accomplished by operation of the push button switch located in the main switch panel. Fuel is transferred from the rear auxiliary tank to the main fuel tanks only. Transfer from the auxiliary fuel tank located beneath the pilots' compartment is accomplished by pumping into the rear auxiliary tank and then into the main fuel tanks, Fuel transfer is automatic upon operation of the fuel transfer switch. Fuel is transferred at unequal rates into the forward fuel tank.

PILOT HEAT CONTROLS

a. Pilot heat is applied by operating the pilot heat switch located in the main switch panel.

WINDSHIELD DEFROSTING

a. Windshield defrosting is accomplished by applying windshield heat through operation of the windshield heater switch.

NAVIGATION LIGHTS

a. The lights are operated by a switch located in the main switch panel.

Section 2 - PILOT OPERATING INSTRUCTIONS

BEFORE ENTERING PILOT"S COMPARTMENT

a. **Flight Restrictions:**
Only normal flying maneuvers should be performed with this airplane until further data is obtained. No high-speed dives should be run.

b. **Air-Speed Limitations:**
The maximum allowable airspeed (IAS) is 950 km/hr (590 mph.)

c. **Center of Gravity Position:**
With the three forward fuel tanks full and the rear one empty, the best center of gravity position will be maintained. This is 156 in. aft of the nose.

d. **Take-off Gross Weight and balance:**
(1) The normal take-off gross weight is 14,272lb, 10,1541b. basic, plus 4118 lb. for fuel, pilot, and ballast.
(2) The most rearward permissible position of the center of gravity is 30% MAC. If this position is exceeded, the airplane becomes unstable about the lateral axis, is apt to yaw about the vertical axis, and automatically stalls in a turn. Under normal conditions of fuel capacity this position is not exceed ed. Refer to fuel through directions.

e. **How to Gain Entrance:**
The cowling on the left hand engine incorporates two steps and a handhold, which permit easy access to the top of the wing. Another step is provided in the fuselage below the cockpit canopy for entry into the cockpit. The central portion of the canopy is hinged along the right hand edge and is raised from the left hand side. It can be locked in place only

from the inside.

ON ENTERING PILOT'S COMPARTMENT

a. Check before all flights:

(1) Check weight and balancc.

(2) Check Form 1.

(3) Diluter lever on "normal oxygen."

(4) Oxygen regulator altitude dial on "normal."

(5) Oxygen pressure 400 to 450 lb. one sq. in.

(6) Set the altimeter and clock.

(7) Battery switch "off"

(8) Generator switches "on".

(9) Pilot heat switch "off."

(10) External power source connected.

b. Special Check for night flying:

(1) Navigation lights.

FUEL SYSTEM MANAGEMENT

a. Fuel Selector Switches:

The fuel valve controls have three positions; rear position fuel shut off; center position rear main fuel tank; and forward position front main fuel tank. In order to maintain a suitable center of gravity, the following selector valve positions have been found to be practical:

(1) When starting the jet units and taxiing: Both fuel selector valves at "rear main fuel tank."

(2) During take-off and in flight: Left hand unit at "front main fuel tank" and right hand unit at "rear main fuel tank." After about ten minutes of flying, switch on the fuel transfer system off the fuel transfer system when the fuel gage shows 900 litres as there may be danger of fuel running over.

b. Fuel Transfer:

Fuel transfer switches are located in the right side of the cockpit, main switch panel.

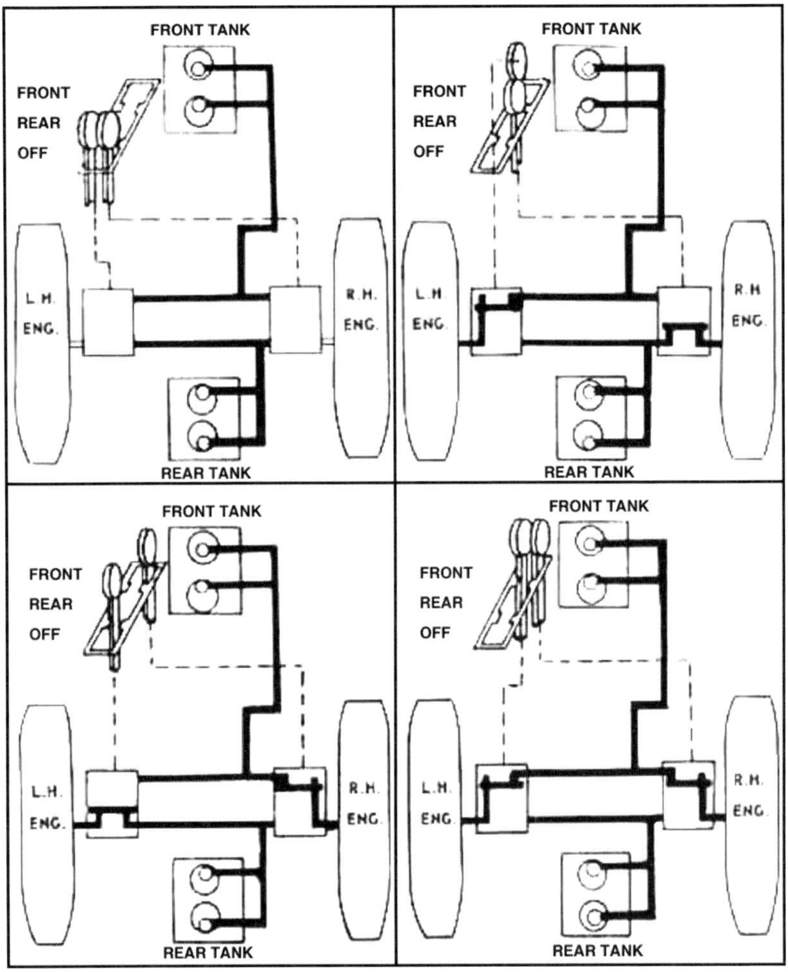

Fuel selector valve positions Me.262

Fuel is pumped from the 53 gal (200 liter) tank to the 158 gal (600 liter) tank and then to the front and rear main tanks. The fuel is pumped into the rear main tank at a faster rate than into the front main tank. The ratio is 3:1.

STARTING PROCEDURES

Warning: All personnel should keep a minimum distance of seven (7) feet from the intake and exhaust openings of the engines.

a. (1) Connect external battery.

(2) Turn on:

(a) Battery switch

(b) Inverter

(c) Generators

Note: Electric fuel pumps are provided and can be used in cold weather conditions when unit is hard to start. These pumps supply gasoline to the burners. They should be shut off when a speed of 3000 rpm is reached.

(3) Turn fuel selector valve "off".

(4) Throttles closed.

(5) Push down starter handle to prime Riedel starting motor.

(6) Pull starter handle and hold; at the same time press tachometer button and hold. This puts tachometer in low speed range.

(7) When jet unit has reached 700 to 800 rpm, press ignition button on right side of throttle and hold. A deep throbbing noise is heard as the unit begins firing. The speed will increase to 1800 to 2000 rpm at this time.

(8) Release starter handle and tachometer button, open fuel selector valve (rear tank position) and slowly advance throttle to 3000 rpm.

(9) At 3000-rpm release throttle ignition button.

b. The jet unit is now running on the main fuel supply. Exhaust temperature must not rise above 650°C. If the jet unit fails to start, release throttle-ignition button. The tail pipe should be wiped clean of any injected fuel before repeating starting process. Otherwise a fire may start. Whenever there is fire or smoke in the turbines, release starter handle at once. Due to this fire hazard, a fire extinguisher should always be ready.

WARM UP AND GROUND TEST

a. Trim stabilizer at 0° tp +1°. With full auxiliary tank use +2° to +3°.

b. Set left engine fuel selector valve on "front tank and right engine fuel selector valve on "rear tank".

c. Set flaps at 20°. Graduations are marked on upper surface of flaps.

d. Open throttles very slowly to 7000 or 8000 rpm. At this speed the needle valve in the tail pipe should move to the fully extended rearward position. This is visible from the cockpit and indicates that maximum thrust is being developed.
e. Check exhaust temperaturc gage for not over 650°C.
f. Check fuel pump pressure gages for 50 to 80 kg/cm2

TAXIING

a. Caution must be used in taxiing because the rudder is ineffective and steering by engine thrust is difficult as thrust builds up too slowly. Brakes are the only means of control, and taxiing should be done with jet units running at 4000 to 6000 rpm. The tail of the ship must not be turned toward inflammable objects.

TAKE-OFF

a. Hold aircraft with main wheel brakes and open throttles very slowly to 7000 rpm.
b. Release brakes and open throttles fully. Make direction al corrections with brakes only. After flying speed (approximately 112 to 125mph [180 to 202 km/hr]) has been attained, pull gently back on stick to raise nose wheel and make the take-off.
c. Apply brakes and retract gear when airborne. Landing gear signal light should indicate wheels in "up" position.
d. Retract flaps airplane will not drop through.

ENGINE FAILURE DURING TAKE-OFF

Note: By opening throttles too fast up to 7000 rpm there is danger of causing cavitation in one of the compressor stages, that is, by running up too quickly the compressor is overloaded and the smooth air flow breaks up just as it does on a stalled wing. If take-off is continued, insufficient air flows through but the same amount of fuel is injected, resulting in insufficient power.

a. If the speed of the aircraft is low, close the throttles and apply the brakes. (Main wheel brakes are foot-operated, nose wheel brake is hand-operated).

b. If already airborne, retract the landing gear as soon as possible, keep the nose down, and use the rudder as necessary to maintain direction until the rudder trim can be adjusted. Continue around the pattern, turning in the direction of the good engine. Minimum single engine speed is 260 km/hr. (160 mph).

CLIMB

The best climbing speeds are given in the take-off and climb chart in Appendix 1.

GENERAL FLYING CHARACTERISTICS

a. Stability

(1) This airplane has good aileron control at all altitudes and will do a good slow roll.

(2) The airplane holds its speed in tight turns much longer than conventional types.

(3) In climbing or turning, automatic slots in the leading edge of the wing open when the speed drops to 450 km/hr. (280 mph). Slots open at 300 km/hr. (185 mph) when the airplane is in a gliding angle.

b. Trim changes:

The stabilizer trim control should not be used when going into or pulling out of a dive. The reason for this is that the entire stabilizer is moved up and down by an electric motor drive actuated by the trim control lever. Thus a slight deflection has a large effect, and it is easy to over-control, causing the ship to nose over or pull up more abruptly than intended.

c. Changing power in flight:

Move the throttles slowly forward or aft.

STALLS

Stalling characteristics are good, there being no bad tendencies to fall off into a spin.

SPINS

No spins are to be attempted with this airplane.

PERMISSABLE ACROBATICS

No acrobatics are to be performed.

DIVING

a. There is reported to be no flutter while diving, possible due to the high position of the horizontal stabilizer in relation to the wing.

b. Speeds of 950 km/hr. (590 mph) are reported to have been attained in a shallow dive 20° to 30° from the horizontal. No vertical dives were made. At speeds of 950 to 1000 km/hr. (590 to 620 mph) the airflow around the aircraft reaches the speed of sound, and it is reported that the control surfaces no longer effect the direction of flight. The results vary with different airplanes; some wing over and dive while others dive gradually. It is also reported that once the speed of sound is exceeded, this condition disappears and normal control is restored.

SPEED AND RANGE

Flight Condition	True Air Speed (Indicated)
Max Speed, 20° to 30° dive	950 km/hr. (590 mph)
Take-off with full fuel load (No bombs)	180 to 202 km/hr. (112 to 127 mph)
Cruising speed	750 km/hr. (465 mph)
Max speed, level flight	830 km/hr. (515 mph)
Landing approach	250 km/hr. (155 mph)
Stalling speed with full fuel load landing gear and flaps down	202 km/hr. (125 mph)

The flight duration of the aircraft varies from 45 to 90 min. Time of flight at low altitudes (below 10,000 to 12,000 ft.) is 45 to 50 min. At altitudes above 12,000 ft. the time of flight is 60 to 90 min. The increased efficiency with altitude is a result of decreased air pressure.

TO TURN OFF JET UNIT DURING FLIGHT

a. Training or test flights:

(1) Close throttle to idling position.

(2) Turn off fuel pump, allowing rpm to decrease.

(3) Fuel selector valve off.

(4) Throttle closed.

(5) Press ignition button throttle for five seconds.

TO START DURING FLIGHT

Do not start above 4 km (13,100 ft.) because of fire hazard.

(1) Reduce airspeed to 300 km/hr. (186mph)

(2) Throttle closed.

(3) Turn on fuel pump.

(4) Press ignition button throttle until rpm increases by 1000.

(5) Open fuel selector valve.

(6) Advance throttle slowly to idling position.

(7) Release ignition button when rpm is constant.

(8) Adjust rpm to that of other unit.

APPROACH AND LANDING

a. Normal landing

Do not lower landing gear above 4000 km/hr. (248 mph). It may be expected that the nose will rise sharply as the landing gear starts down, but once the wheels are in landing position the aircraft will assume a normal attitude by retrimming stabilizer.

The landing approach is made at 250 km/hr. (155 mph). Use flaps as needed and carry 6000 to 7000 rpm so that throttles can be opened quickly in case of a go-around.

Note: If rpm is less than 6000, any advance in throttles must be made slowly to 7000 rpm before opening wide. The airplane stalls at 180 to 202 km/hr. (112 to 125 mph). In case of a very short flight in which the fuel has not all been used from the auxiliary tanks, use caution in landing as the allowable landing weight is exceeded due to the fuel load.

b. Take-off if landing is not completed:

(1) If 6000 to 7000 rpm or over has been maintained on the approach, open throttles fully in going around.

Note: If rpm has fallen below 6000 it is necessary to bring the units up to 6000 to 7000 rpm slowly, just as in take-off, before opening throttlcs.

(2) Brake and retract landing gear.

(3) Gradually raise flaps to take-off setting of 20°.

STOPPING UNITS

(1) Close throttles completely and press ignition buttons.

(2) Shut off fuel selector valves.

(3) Open fuel dump valve switches.

In the event that power units should begin to burn, pull starter handles, re-ignite power plant and then repeat above shutting down process.

BEFORE LEAVING THE PILOT'S COMPARTMENT

Turn all switches off.

Section 3 – FLIGHT OPERATING DATA

ENGINE OPERATING DATA

Condition	Exhaust Gas Temperature	Fuel Pump pressure
Maximum	650°C	80kg/cm2
Maximum	—	50kg/cm2

Operating Condition	RPM	Time Limit
Take-off	8700 +/- 200	5 min
Military	8700 +/- 200	10 min
Max continuous (90%)	8400	—

Airplane Model M2-262 A-1

- Minimum: Fuel Grade Jet
- Engines: AN-F-32
- Riedel Starters: AN-F-32 (with % pt of engine oil added to

each gallon).

- Oil Grade: AAF Spec. No. 3606

AIR SPEED CORRECTION DATA

(Information not available pending flight tests)

Section 4 – EMERGENCY OPERATING INSTRUCTIONS

FLIGHT ON ONE JET UNIT

a. The aircraft will fly at 450 to 500km/hr. (280 to 310 mph) on one jet unit. It operates best over 3km (10,000 ft.).
b. The minimum single engine speed of 260 km/hr. can only be reached by climbing too steeply or with landing gear down.
c. Bank only in the direction of the good jet unit unless speeds over 260km/hr. are maintained.

EMERGENCY SHUTDOWN OF JET UNIT DURING FLIGHT

a. Jerk throttle closed.
b. Turn fuel pump off.
c. Turn fuel selector valve off.

EMERGENCY OPERATION OF LANDING GEAR AND FLAPS

a. Compressed air is used for emergency operation. It lowers the nose wheel and main landing gear fairing. The main gear falls and locks by the influence of gravity. If it does not immediatcly lock it can be helped by side- slipping. Both the landing gear and the flaps lower more quickly by the use of compressed air than hydraulically. The main gear goes down in 2 to 3 sec and the nose wheel goes down in 5 to 10 sec. **Note:** Two to three turns of the air valve are necessary to put compressed air into operation.

TIRE BLOWOUT DURING TAKE-OFF OR LANDING

a. Keep the airplane straight by using corresponding throttles and applying opposite brakes until the airplane comes to a stop.

BAIL –OUT

a. Pull the emergency handle for cockpit canopy release. Bail out to the one side. Wait approximately two seconds before pulling the ripcord.

LANDING WITH ONE JET UNIT

a. Approach the field, turning in the direction of the good jet unit.
b. Lower the landing gear by compressed air (two complete turns of air valve) when 3 to 4 km (2 to 2.5 miles) out on the landing approach. Main gear goes down in 2 to 3 sec and the nose wheel goes down in 5 to 10 sec.
c. Lower flaps as needed, as the airplane will not go around again on one jet unit.
d. When the landing gear has been lowered by compressed air, the landing gear down button must be pressed when the jet units are running, before the next take-off.

POSSIBLE FAILURES OF THE ENGINES IN STARTING AND IN FLIGHT

a. In Starting

(1) The Riedel Motor Does Not Start:
The electro-motor in the Riedel is turning the jet unit over slowly. The voltage should read 20 v, in which case do not use the starter switch for more than 10 sec to avoid burning out the electro-motor.

(2) The Riedel motor sounds as if it were running, but no rpm is indicated with the tachometer in the low-speed range.

(a) Tachometer inoperative
(b) Starter claw is broken

(3) The ignition does not respond immediately; press the ignition button several times. If ignition finally takes place, long flames will come out of the jet unit. This will also

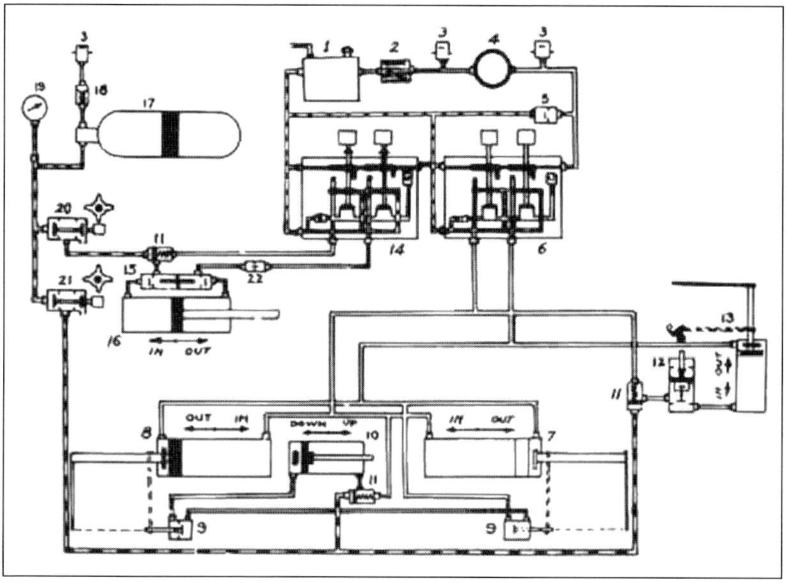

1. Hydraulic fluid reservoir 2. Segment filter 3. External connection 4. Hydraulic fluid pump 5. Pressure relief valve 6. Wheel distributor valve 7. R.H. wheel cylinder 8. L.H. wheel cylinder 9. Limit cylinder 10. Wheel flaps cylinder 11. Exchange valve (emergency) 13. Nose wheel limit cylinder 14. Nose wheel cylinder 15. Landing flap distributor valve 15. Double-acting valve 16. Landing flaps cylinder 17. Compressed air bottle 18. Check valve 19. Pressure gauge 20. Emergency valve for landing flaps 21. Emergency valve for wheels 22. Throttling valve

happen if fuel has previously run into the jet unit. These flames will blow out.

(4) The ignition is accidentally turned on when the jet unit is stopped, and flames come out of the unit. The ignition should be released and the Riedel motor started so that the air flow will extinguish the flames. If the Riedel motor is not used, a mechanic can either blow compressed air through the front or use a fire extinguisher at the rear.

b. In Flight.

(1) Jet unit is extinguished - indicated by:

(a) Drop in rpm.

(b) Drop in fuel pressure.

(c) Drop in gas pressure.

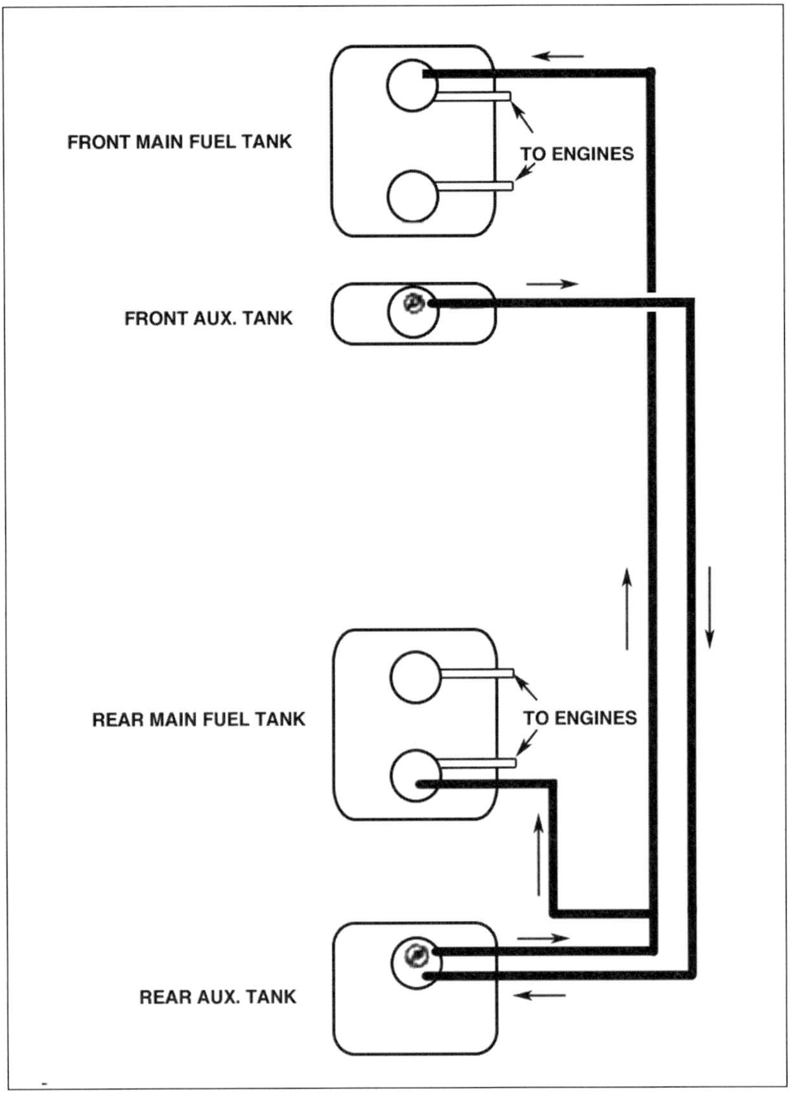

Fuel transfer systems Me.262

(d) Drop in tail-pipe gas temperature and trailing of white smoke.

Causes:

(a) Throttle pulled back further than idling position.

(b) Stoppage of fuel supply

(c) Insufficient injection pressure at high altitudes.

(2) Broken vanes in jet unit:

Indicated by: Vibration of the unit.

Action: Turn off the jet to prevent the fuel lines from breaking and causing a fire.

(3) Damaged turbine starter vanes:

Indicated by:

(a) Fuel pressure increases rapidly.

(b) Gas pressure increases rapidly.

(c) Gas temperature increases rapidly.

Action: Turn off the jet unit immediately to avoid fire.

(4) Injection nozzle clogged:

Indicated by:

(a) Fuel pressure increases rapidly.

(b) Gas temperature is abnormally high or low.

Action: Turn off the jet unit immediately to avoid fire.

(5) Loss of oil or oil pump inoperative:

Indicated by:

(a) RPM surges upward.

(b) Gas temperature rises to the limit of gage.

Action: Turn off the jet unit immediately to avoid fire.

(6) Thrust governor inoperative or the nozzle pin adjustment broken, in either case the thrust nozzle pin advances to the final notch:

Indicated by:

(a) Fuel pressure increases rapidly.

(b) Gas pressure increases rapidly.

(c) Gas temperature increases rapidly.

Action: Turn off the jet unit immediately avoid fire.

(7) Landing gear retraction trouble:

(a) If the landing gear does not come up when the button is again pressed, reduce the speed to 160 mph and suddenly push down the nose.

(b) If the signal lamp does not work, there traction of the landing gear can be checked as follows:

(1) If a slight rush of air is heard and the speed is 405

to 435 mph, the nose wheel is still down.

(2) If a strong rush of air is heard and the speed is 280 to 310 mph, the entire landing gear is still down.

Section 5 – OPERATIONAL EQUIPMENT

HEATING AND VENTILATING

a. Heating of the cock pit is obtained by operation of the control marked "cabin heat"

b. Ventilating is accomplished by opening a small air scoop on the upper left of the fuselage just forward of the canopy. The scoop is operated by means of a control lever.

OXYGEN SYSTEM

a. This is a standard low-pressure oxygen system with a diluter demand oxygen pressure-breathing regulator, Type A-14.

b. Normal oxygen pressure is 400 to 450 lb./sq. in.

ARMAMENT A.

Not applicable.

COMMUNICATIONS EQUIPMENT

a. The airplane has a standard installation of an SCR-522 transmitter and receiver with a BC-602A control box.

APPENDIX ONE

Flight Altitudes	True Climbing Speeds (Indicated)
0 to 4 km (0 to 13000ft)	climb at 450km/hr. (279mph)
4 to 6 km (13000 – 19700ft)	climb at 500km/hr. (310mph)
6 to 8 km (19700 – 26200ft)	climb at 550km/hr. (342 mph)
8 to 10 km (26200 – 32800 ft)	climb at 600-650 km/hr. (372-403 mph)

Note: The German airspeed indicator registers true airspeed, above 400 km/hr., due to altitude compensation in the instrument.

ITEMS OF TYPICAL LOADING

- Oil - 4.5 Gallons At Stations 100.13

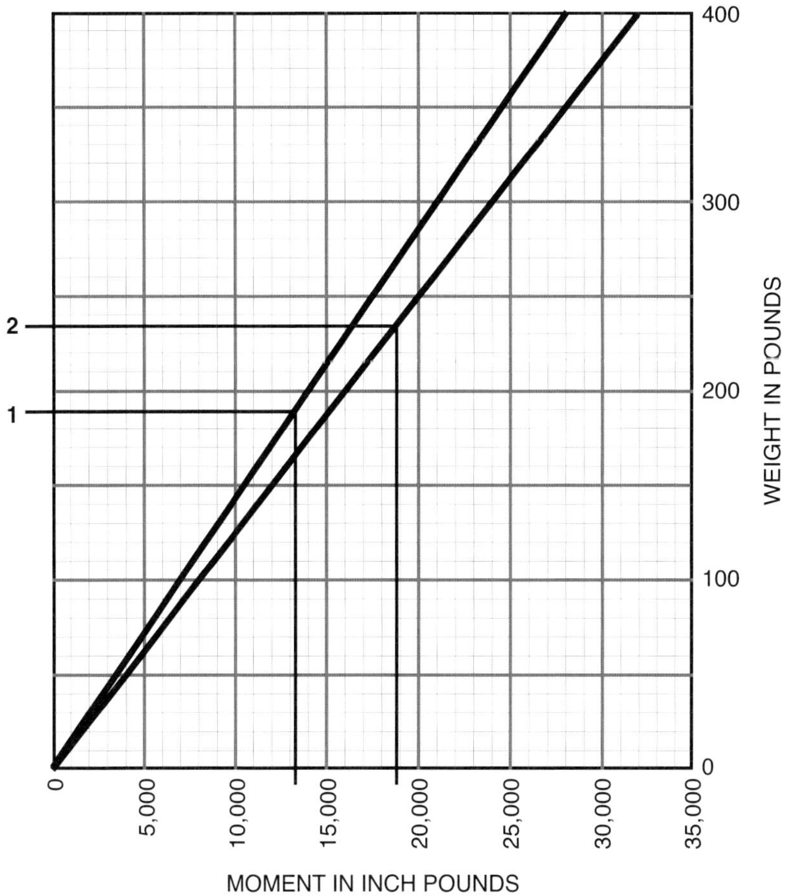

AMMUNITION AND BALLAST GRAPH ME.262

1. Front ammunition box - lower guns - 160 rounds capacity

2. Rear ammunition box - upper guns - 200 rounds capacity

Forward ammunition box - Fuselage Station 70.50

Rearward ammunition box - Fuselage Station 79.19

Unit weights of Mark 108 ammunition

AP/I/T-8253 Grains - 1.1768 lbs

HE/T-4492 Grains - .6209 lbs

AP/HE/T-7532 Grains - 1.0733 lbs

AP-5408 Grains - .7710 lbs

- Pilot And Chute - 200lb At Station 163.9
- Fuel - See Fuel Graph
- Ammunition - See Ammunition And Ballast Graph
- Ballast - See Ammunition And Ballast Graph

<table>
<tr><th rowspan="2">Container</th><th rowspan="2">Station</th><th rowspan="2">Weight</th><th colspan="2">Capacity</th></tr>
<tr><th>Gallons</th><th>Liters</th></tr>
<tr><td>1 Front main tank</td><td>111.5</td><td>1593</td><td>238</td><td>900</td></tr>
<tr><td>2 Front auxiliary tank</td><td>137.75</td><td>354</td><td>53</td><td>200</td></tr>
<tr><td>3 Rear main tank</td><td>207.5</td><td>1593</td><td>238</td><td>900</td></tr>
<tr><td>4 Rear auxiliary tank</td><td>242.5</td><td>1062</td><td>159</td><td>600</td></tr>
<tr><td>5 Jettisonable tanks-2</td><td>93.61</td><td>1062</td><td>159</td><td>600</td></tr>
</table>

Fuel unit weight - 6.7 lbs/gal

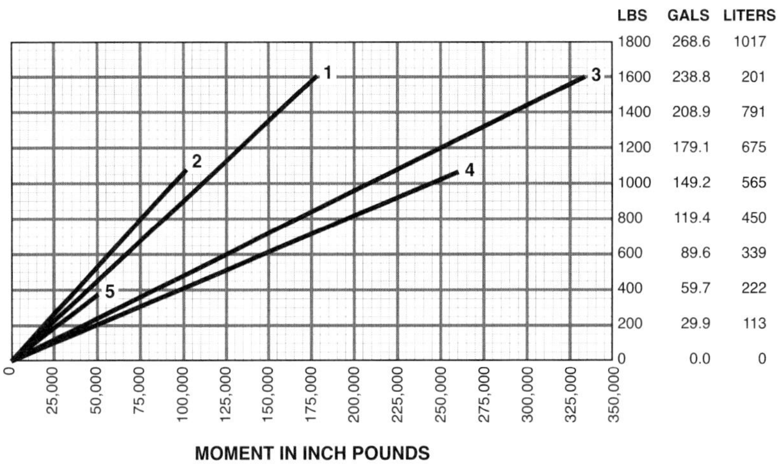

FUEL LOADING TABLE AND GRAPH ME.262

- Jettisonable Tanks - (Two) 66 Lb. At Station 93.31
- Jettisonable Tank Hanging Fittings - 22lb. At Station 93.31

To derive center of gravity in percent of mean aerodynamic chord: arm - 138-43 x 100 = %MAC 76.06

NOTE:

- Most forward allowable center of gravity is 18.5% MAC.
- Most rearward allowable center of gravity is 30% MAC

PILOTS NOTES ON ME.262 BY FLUG KAPITAN WENDEL

A.1.2,(G) REPORT NO. 2357

HANDLING THE Me.262

Several Me.262 aircraft have been captured intact and will be flown by Allied test pilots. In view of this some notes which have been obtained from the Offices of Messerschmitt at Augsburg have been translated by this section and are reproduced below.

In addition to studying the condensed instructions for airframe and engines, a thorough knowledge of these notes, preferably before the first flight in an Me.262, is essential to the pilot.

1. Taxiing

Always accelerate the engines slowly. The gas temperature must never rise above the permitted value and the engine must not "roar" (bullern). In view of this, only take corners by using the brakes, never by using the engines. Always taxi gently and never make sharp turns, otherwise control of the aircraft will be lost.

2. Take-off

Switch on the fuel pumps in the main tanks. Hold the aircraft stationary by applying the brakes and then slowly run up the engines, especially slowly up to 7,500 rpm. The brakes must be so adjusted that they will hold the aircraft stationary up to 8,500 rpm.

After releasing the brakes, push the throttle lever right forward and then check over the engine. The aircraft makes so little demand upon the pilot at the commencement of the take-off run that he is easily able to carry out this check. The check is done by eye and ear, the engines must not "roar" and the instruments must show the same values as they did during running up or during previous take-off's. The gas pressure must be especially watched, and if it is more than five per cent lower than previously, do not take-off. In such a case, it is most likely that cavitation has taken place in one of the compressor stages, that is, by running up too quickly, the compressor has been overloaded and the smooth flow breaks up, exactly as it does when a wing stalls. Cavitation takes place so easily in many compressors as a result of small constructional faults or as a result of foreign bodies that they become entirely unserviceable. If the take-off is continued when cavitation has occurred in the compressor, then the quantity of air flowing through is too small, the quantity of fuel injected however is the same or sometimes even larger, as a result of which, the engine is overheated.

The directional corrections during take-off should only be made with the brakes.The control column should remain in the neutral position.

The angle of attack of the wing, when running on all three wheels, is smaller than the angle of attack when flying at the lowest possible speed (after becoming airborne).

As a result of this, when the aircraft has reached the lowest permissible flying speed, the angle of attack must be increased, in other words, the aircraft must be pulled away from the ground. If the stick is pulled back too soon, or if, at the right speed, it is pulled back too far, then there is only a rise in resistance, but no increase in lift, in fact, there may be lessening of it. The aircraft cannot then climb. In this case immediately reduce the angle of attack to the "running" angle, in other words, push the stick forward and then start the process again.

When will the aircraft be pulled off the ground? It is best to go by the A.S.I, which should read with a fighter, fully laden i.e. 6,700 kg., 190 - 200 kph. with a bomber, fully laden i.e. 7,100 kg., 200 - 220 kph. After becoming airborne, immediately push the stick forward slightly as the required elevator angle for pulling off the ground is greater than that for climbing at the slowest speed.

Essential for a perfect take-off is correct setting of the tailplane. The tailplane must always be trimmed nose heavy! The further back the center of gravity moves, the more nose heavy it must be trimmed. When the 600 liter fuel tank is full, the center of gravity is at its rearmost position. The tailplane must then be set at +2x - +3 (i.e 4-6 graduations on the indicator).

3. Rocket Take-Off

In order to shorten the take-off run, the rockets should be ignited 40 - 30 kph. before the optimum take-off speed. If the take-off run need not be shorter, but there are obstacles to be negotiated after becoming airborne, then only ignite the rockets later, possibly even leaving it until the aircraft is airborne. Jettison the take-off rockets at low speeds; otherwise damage may be caused to the fuselage.

4. Operation of undercarriage and landing flaps

The undercarriage and landing flaps are hydraulically operated. The hydraulic pump has a capacity of 18 litres/min. and is attached to the port engine. Its capacity is rather too low and it is intended to fit an 18 litre per minute pump on the starboard engine. In the present state, therefore, the undercarriage operates very slowly. This is particularly noticeable when lowering. The nose wheel comes down very much later than the main undercarriage; so lower in plenty of time. The high speed of the aircraft easily tempts one to lower the undercarriage of flaps whilst travelling too fast and this leads to damage. The permissible operating speed must be rigidly adhered to.

5. Emergency operation

Compressed air is used for emergency operation of the undercarriage and it lowers the nose wheel and the main undercarriage fairing. The undercarriage itself falls under the influence of gravity. If it does not immediately lock, then assist it by sideslipping.

6. Warning

The compressed air is only admitted to the undercarriage or flaps after two full turns of the operating handle have been made. With emergency operation both undercarriage and flaps lower more quickly.

7. Flight

Always climb at optimum climbing speed, never more slowly. The best speeds are given in the table below:

Altitude	Speed
0 m.	475 kph. (true)
2,000 m.	500 kph. (true)
4,000 m.	525 kph. (true)
6,000 m.	550 kph. (true)
8,000 m.	600 kph. (true)
10,000 m.	650 kph. (true)

Note: The Me.262 has an altitude compensated A.S.I, and, therefore, the indicated speed is equivalent to the true speed above 400 kph. The highest permissible rearward point for the center of gravity is 30 percent of the mean aerodynamic wing chord. If this position is exceeded, then the aircraft becomes unstable about the lateral axis, that is, it does not remain trimmed, but will automatically stall in a turn.

Under normal conditions of fuel stowage, this position is not exceeded, but it is necessary always to watch most carefully the transfer pumping instructions. Watch particularly that the main tanks do not overflow as the J-2 fuel will run out into the fuselage and get on the wifeless equipment, which interferes with no radio traffic.

When cruising, the tailplane must be between 0 and +2.

8. Directional Stability

When the center of gravity is far back and the Flettner rudder trimming tabs are not perfect, especially if the Flettner tabs are a little too thick, then the aircraft sways about the vertical axis. This movement must stop when both legs are pushed hard against the rudder pedals. If this does not stop the movement then the tabs must be altered or the trailing edge of the rudder must be bent slightly outwards. A modification is in course of preparation.

9. Landing

The best approach speed is 230 - 250 kph. Shortly before reaching the airfield boundary, decrease the glide angle a little and reduce the speed to about 200 kph. Then flatten out and touch down normally as with an aircraft having a tail wheel. Touch-down speed is 175 kph. After touch- down, allow the aircraft to tip forward slowly. Only apply brakes when the nose wheel has touched the ground.

10. Going round again

It is just as easy to go round again as with other types of aircraft, but is must be remembered that by approaching slowly the engine revolutions are low, and just as at take-off, the throttle lever must only be moved forward slowly.

11. Single Engine Flight

When flying on one engine only, a turning moment is developed about the vertical axis, due to the engine being offset from the longitudinal axis of the aircraft. The amount of this moment is dependent upon the power and the leverage. In this case the leverage remains constant, but the power (i.e. the effect of the running engine) changes. In order that the aircraft may remain on course, this moment must be offset, which is done by applying rudder. The amount of rudder applied must be sufficient to keep the ball of the turn and bank indicator in the center; note this particularly in turns. Turns can be made either with or against the stationary engine. During long single-engine flights the force on the rudder pedal may be reduced by adjusting the Flettner trimming tabs.

The turning moment imparted by the specific movement of the rudder is dependent on airflow pressure. The smaller the pressure, the greater must be the rudder movement. In single-engine flight, with retracted undercarriage, the speed is something over 500 kph. at full throttle. In this case only about y$ of the possible rudder movement is necessary. This low speed, however, can only occur at full throttle if one is climbing at too great an angle or if the undercarriage has been lowered.

12. Single Engine landings

From what has previously been said, it will be seen that the following is necessary for a single-engine landing; minimum approach speed 260 kph., so that, if necessary, full throttle may be given. At this speed and with one engine at full throttle, the aircraft loses height with lowered undercarriage, but raised flaps at 1 - 2 Ms./sec. From this, it will be seen that the undercarriage should only be lowered at such a time that it is possible to reach the airfield with little or no aid from the engine. Approach speed 260 kph. About 500ms. before reaching the airfield (when too high earlier, when too low later) lower the flaps and complete the landing in a normal manner. Side slipping is possible. When landing, the Flettner trimming tabs should be set in the neutral position. If it is necessary to approach under power, then the pilot must exert the necessary force on the rudder. At full throttle under all circumstances apply full rudder.

25th May, 1945
H.G. MORISON
Squadron Leader for Wing Commander

FLYING THE Me.262 IN COMBAT

With Allied aircraft operating in ever-increasing numbers over the Reich, operational evaluation of the Me.262 had been difficult, to say the least. Trying to work the bugs out of an aircraft while dodging enemy fighters was far from an ideal situation for flight test.

The evaluation did show that the Me.262 was not only fast but was responsive and docile. However, it did tend to "snake" at high speeds, reducing its accuracy as a gun platform, and it was underpowered, with a long take-off run. Losing an engine was very dangerous, since the Me.262 could barely stay in the air on one engine. If an engine was lost below 290 KPH (180 MPH), the aircraft would usually be lost as well. The engines were also not very reliable, being prone to flameouts and burnouts.

As we have seen the first documented air combat involving an Me.262 took place on 25 July 1944, when a Schwalbe pounced on an RAF Mosquito that escaped. One Me.262 was shot down near Brussels on 28 August by a pair of USAAF P-47 Thunderbolts, the first Me.262 to be lost to direct enemy action. An operational fighter squadron, the "Kommando Nowotny", was established out of Erprobungskommando 262 in September 1944, under experienced ace Major Walter Nowotny. Kommando Nowotny became operational on 3 October.

The Me.262 was highly vulnerable on take-off and landing since the Jumo engines took a long time to throttle up; since the engines tended to set asphalt runways on fire, the Me.262 was restricted to operations at airfields with concrete runways, which were more easily targeted by the Allies than dispersed dirt airfields. On 7 October two were shot down on take-off by Lieutenant Urban L. Drew of the USAAF, flying a P-51 Mustang. The Luftwaffe eventually assigned FW-190s, when they were available and had fuel, to fly air patrols around the air bases to protect the Me.262s, and the airfields were ringed by heavy flak defences. The flak installations were a mixed blessing, however, since they were often staffed by poorly trained and nervous troops who were just as likely to fire on friends as foes.

Many of the Me.262 pilots were also inexperienced, and flying an aircraft with performance greater than any operated before would have been a challenge to more professional aviators. Hitting Allied bombers while streaking through a formation at high speed was difficult, and if an Me.262 pilot slowed down to take more careful aim, he became a good target for the bombers' defensive fire and escorting Allied fighters.

Attrition was high. Nowotny himself was killed in action on 8 November 1944 when his and two other Me.262s were shot down. The few survivors were incorporated into a full Me.262 group, "III/JG7", which achieved a number of kills in the months remaining of the war. Two other groups, "I/JG7" and "II/JG7" were never fully brought up to strength. Four more bomber units were formed but saw little action.

Faced with overwhelming Allied strength and extreme logistical problems, particularly fuel shortages, Me.262 operations during those months were intermittent. An elite unit, "JV-44", was formed up under Adolf Galland, and racked up a number of kills before hostilities ended. Many of these kills were achieved with the new R4M 55mm (2.2 inch) folding fin rockets. An Me.262 could carry a total of 24 such weapons on wooden racks, one under each wing, and if fired into a bomber formation the rockets could have a devastating effect on anything they hit. Schwalbes configured to carry the R4M were given the

A B-24 Liberator shot down by an Me.262

designation "Me.262A-1b".

A ground-attack version of the R4M rocket was also designed and might have helped turn the Me.262 into an effective "Jabo" aircraft, much like the RAF's rocket-firing Typhoons or "Rockoons", but it does not appear the Luftwaffe ever used the Me.262 in this way.

THE Me.262 ACES

A flying ace or fighter ace is a military aviator credited with shooting down five or more enemy aircraft during aerial combat (The Germans traditionally set the threshold at 10 victories.) During World War II hundreds of German Luftwaffe fighter pilots achieved this feat flying contemporary piston engine fighter aircraft. However, only 28 pilots are credited with shooting down five or more enemy aircraft while flying a jet-powered aircraft.

Jet aircraft made their World War II combat debut when Lieutenant Alfred Schreiber, flying Messerschmitt Me.262 A-1a W.Nr. 130 017 (German language: Werknummer - factory number), attacked a No. 540 Squadron Royal Air Force

Mosquito PR XVI (a photo-reconnaissance aircraft) over the Alps on 26 July 1944.

Although often referred to as the first aerial victory by a jet fighter in aviation history, the damaged Mosquito actually managed to return to an Allied airfield in Italy. The first jet victory was therefore the confirmed destruction of another No. 540 Squadron reconnaissance Mosquito PR XVI, which was shot down by Leutnant Joachim Weber over Ohlstadt on 8 August 1944.

By 1944-45 the German Luftwaffe committed three new types of jet- or rocket-propelled fighters to combat operations. Besides the Me.262, the rocket propelled Me 163 "Komet" and the He 162 "Volksjäger" had become operational. Although a few claims were made by pilots of the Me 163 and He 162, no pilot achieved ace status on either of these two types.

***

The problem for the Luftwaffe is the fact that it was not possible to get enough of the new generation of fighters into the air, and this study of German Air Tactics Against Ground Targets in the Third U.S. Army Area confirms the comparative rarity of the Me.262.

1. Prior to the allied landings of the continent, 6 June 1944, a great deal already was known of the tactics of the German Air Force in attacking ground targets. Attacks of appreciable size had occurred in Italy and Sicily and along the North African coast, and some time had been devoted to their study. Targets of opportunity in forward areas received 63% of attacks, highways and bridges received but 4% of attention, and ports and harbors, airfields and ammunition dumps received 33%, 55% of attacks were by dive-bombing, 20% level-bombing, 10% strafing, 12% unknown, and 3% reconnaissance flights. Bombers made much use of cloud cover and the blinding effect of the bright sun in making their approaches to the target areas. In brief, strong, close-in defenses of all vital objectives seemed dictated by past

Luftwaffe performances, with forward zones of divisions, and roads and bridges being of prime importance. An adequate alert status and an efficient warning system were necessary to guard against surprise.

2. Experiences in Italy were, to a certain extent, repeated during the course of Third U.S. Army's operations on the continent from 1 August 1944 to 8 May 1945. Thus, during periods of rapid and threatening advance, armored spearheads were continually attacked by large numbers of low-flying aircraft which attempted to blunt their thrusts. As rivers were reached, emphasis turned to attacks upon the bridges and crowded bridge areas. It the air effort was particularly large, much of it spilled over into troop and artillery areas of infantry divisions following the armor. Little if any air activity was encountered behind corps rear boundaries during such times. Sole large-scale exception to this was during the initial break-through drive of Third U.S. Army's VIII Corps down the Cotentin Peninsula. During that period, from 1 August to 12 August 1944, the GAF made a frenzied effort that struck night and day not only at the spearheading armor and motorized infantry, but at bridges, road defiles, dams and antiaircraft behind them up and down the historic Avranches supply route Thus, targets were chosen because of their vital importance, and merely vulnerable targets, such as supply dumps, airfields, and the like were left almost untouched.

3. During periods of comparatively little forward movement, such as occurred along the Moselle River in France, there were few attacks made but, weather permitting, reconnaissance was flown almost daily over division and corps zones while some nuisance strafing and bombing of artillery positions occurred.

4. The only time this over-all pattern varied was during the German break-through effort in Luxembourg and Belgium in the First U.S. Army sector. As Third U.S. Army withdrew its divisions from its own line and turned north to strike at the south

flank of the German bulge, the Luftwaffe for the first time penetrated deeply into the army area behind corps rear boundaries. Supply installations, bridges, railway supply trains, troop assemblies and convoys, CPs—all were bombed and strafed while at the same time close support was furnished German panzer units by attacks upon our artillery, tanks and beleaguered garrisons, such as at Bastogne, Belgium. Several nuisance attacks and one large-scale attack was made on airfields in the army area. In addition, many reconnaissance sorties were flown. A comparison of figures shows that while the Hun was on the defensive, approximately 20% of air activity occurred behind corps boundaries, but that during the counter-offensive approximately 40% of all sorties were reported behind corps, and this at a time when the Army had four corps instead of the usual two or three.

5. It is difficult to state altitudes at which attacks were made since many attacks combined several tactics, and strafing frequently followed bombing. For the entire course of the army's operations, 2,463 raids by 6,192 enemy aircraft were reported by AAA sources. Of these, 1,226 raids developed into actual attacks, the remaining raids being for reconnaissance or unknown purposes. A graphical presentation of types of attacks appears below. The type of attack was unknown on 3.7% of the 1,226 raids involving attacks.

6. A total of 6,192 enemy aircraft were over the entire army area of which AAA gunners engaged 4,985. The remaining 1,207 airplanes were observed but not fired upon for various reasons, such as being out of range, etc. However, many of these 4,985 aircraft were seen and engaged by several units in succession. The tabulation opposite tallies German aircraft as they were separately observed and reported by the various AAA battalions. Screening to eliminate duplicate reports of the same airplanes has not been done.

7. Tactics of attacking aircraft varied considerably but some

Frequency of Engagements by Plane Types		Claims	
		Cat I	**Cat II**
3043	Me-109	426	225
2267	FW 190	296	174
377	Ju-88	35	29
359	Me-262	22	21
134	Me-210 and Me-410	10	5
56	He-111	7	9
40	Ar-234	2	1
38	Me-110	8	3
27	Ju-87	3	1
16	Ju-188	2	2
11	Ju-52	4	1
10	Do-217	3	1
9	Bu-181	7	0
4	Me-108	2	1
4	Me-163	0	0
3	FW-200	1	1
3	Fi-156	1	0
2	He-177	1	0
2	Hs-126	0	0
1	Go-145	1	0
2747	Unknown	276	106
40	Obsn and Trng Types	16	3
11	Jet-propelled types	0	0
Unfiltered Total = 9204	**Unfiltered Claims**	**1123**	**583**
Filtered Total = 6192	**Approved Claims**	**927**	**279**

generalities may be stated. Thus, while enemy pilots took advantage of a low sun in making attacks at dusk and dawn no preference for these particular hours was shown and attacks were spread throughout periods of the day and night. Cloud cover also was used where available. Attacking planes tended to fly closer to the ground toward the end of the war, thus hoping to defeat radar early warning facilities and also to reduce time within range of light AAA weapons. There were no massed bombing attacks attempted. Individual tactics and ruses were noted as follows:

(a) "Window" was occasionally dropped in large quantities but on only one occasion did it make radar tracking of airplanes impossible.

(b) Enemy aircraft cut their motors to glide silently toward a target, thus, hoping to escape detection.

(c) Enemy aircraft made little use of tracer ammunition in their night strafing attacks.

(d) Some E/A flew in low to attract light AAA fire, even turning their landing lights on for this purpose. When fire was opened from the ground, other planes at higher altitudes and out of range bombed the disclosed positions.

(e) Most attacks were by E/A attacking one, two, or three at a time. In raids involving 50-75 airplanes, the formations broke up into smell elements of 2 to 4 planes, attacking from all directions.

(f) E/A engaged in mock dogfights, leading ground troops to believe a allied aircraft were pursuing German aircraft.

(g) Rocket-firing techniques appeared to be to dive at an angle of 45°, releasing the rockets at 500-1,000 ft. altitude.

(h) Most frequently used evasive maneuver, when engaged by AAA, was to dive low and level off near the ground. In avoiding AW fire, violent turns were used, or planes dropped to hedge-hopping levels. Bursts of speed also were employed. Those E/A which tried to climb or make bank turns were often shot down, except where they climbed to cloud cover or directly into the sun.

***

One often-overlooked fact is the logistical difficulties of the ground. After the war Adolf Galland expanded on the subject during interrogation.

Jet aircraft like the Me.262 needed special concrete aprons at the end of the runways where they could be lined up for a scramble, since they had great difficulty in taxiing. Another problem for all units was the great shortage of tugs for towing aircraft. It was best to have one tug per aircraft, but units had to scrape to have even two per three aircraft. The strength of conventional fighter units went up sharply in fall 1944, and made this shortage more serious. Despite all efforts to build new fields and improve old ones, the shortage became worse and worse. Those fields, which were built or improved, usually near the fronts, were continually, over-run. In 1945 there was a great shortage of jet airfields even though jet strength was very low.

Protection of Me. 262 Airfields:

Little was done in the way of construction of bunkers or underground hangers. Light Flak was depended on for protection against low level attacks. Galland believes it to have been very effective. Each airfield of any importance had its own Flak Kompanie under the Luftgau. Small caliber weapons of all kinds were used, including numbers of 50cal. guns from American bombers. Most fields had over 200 guns and at Munchen/Reim there were 270. Jets like the Me.262 required much Flak protection, well spread out at distances from the airfield, because the aircraft were very slow in landing and takeoff and required good protection.

Me.262 Training:

Following his usual policy, Galland wanted to allot the first Me.262's to the operational units and convert them to the new fighter during ongoing operations to save time. Then, he would have supplied the OTUs and, last, the fighter schools. But he was only able to do this in the case of J.G.7. The bomber units got most of the rest of the Me.262s. III/Erg. Jagd Geschwader 2 was the OTU for the Me.262. It was next equipped, but the program never got much farther. No drastic changes in training were contemplated.

PILOTS OF THE ME.262

Walter Nowotny

Walter Nowotny was born on 7 December at Gmund. He joined the Luftwaffe on October 1st, 1939. In 1941 he scored his first victories near the island of Osel, located in the Baltic by shooting down three I-153s. However, he was hit in combat and had to ditch his aircraft over the sea. He spent three days in his dinghy, using his hands as paddles, until he reached land. He was awarded the Knight's Cross of the Iron Cross after scoring his 56th victory on 4 September 1942 - four weeks after shooting down seven Russian aircraft in a single day. On the 25th October 1942, and 21 years old, Nowotny was promoted to command 9./JG 54. It was a momentous promotion, as JG 54, the famous "Green Hearts", was one of Luftwaffe's most powerful fighter units.

He scored nine kills on August 13th of 1943, and then scored seven more on the 21st. During September 1943, his total of kills reached 200. He received the Oak leaves and Swords on September 22nd and became the 37th holder of these awards. By mid-October 1943 he won 250 victories, becoming the first pilot in history to reach that number. He then received the Diamonds, becoming the youngest ever (at 22 years old) and only eighth recipient of this, Germany's highest military award.

His career was temporarily put on hold when he was assigned command of Schulegeschwader (SJG) 101, a training unit for

Pilot	Me262 Kills	Total Kills	Last Unit
Maj. Georg-Peter Eder	24	78	III JG7
Oblt. Kurt Welter	20+	56	NJG 11
Obstl. Heinz Bar	18	221	JV44
Hptm. Franz Schall	16	133	III JG7
Lt. Rudolf Rademacher	16+	97	III JG7
Maj. Erich Rudorffer	12	224	III JG7
Lt. Hermann Buchner	12	58	III JG7
Lt. Karl Schnorrer	11	46	III JG7
Lt. Heinz Lennartz	9	11	III JG7
Lt. Fritz Muller	9	22	III JG7
Maj. Theodor Weissenberger	8	208	JG7
Maj. Heinrich Ehrler	8	208	JG7
Oblt. Walter Schuck	8	206	JG7
Oblt. Gunther Wegmann	8	21	JG7
Obfw. Erich Buttner	8	8	III JG7
Lt. Hans Dieter Weihs	8	8	JG7
Genlt. Adolph Galland	7	104	JV44
Ofw. Heinz Arnold	7	49	JG7
Lt. Alfred Ambs	7	7	JG7
Flwb. Karl-Heinz Becker	7	7	NJG 11
Unteroff. Franz Koster	7	7	JV44
Obst. Johannes Steinhoff	6	178	JV44
Obst. Hans Stehle	6	?	JG7
Lt. Alfred Schreiber	6	6	III JG7
Lt. Joachim Weber	6	?	III JG7
Maj. Wolfgang Spate	5	99	III JG7
Obst. Hans Grunberg	5	82	JV44
Fhr. Friedrich Ehrig	5	?	JG7
Lt. Bruno Mischkot	5	7	JG7
Lt. Klaus Neumann	5	37	JV44
Oberfw. Helmut Baudach	5	20	JG7
Maj. Walter Nowotny	2	258	KN
Obst. Gunther Lutzow	2	110	JV44
Hpt. Walter Krupinski	2	197	JV44
Obst. Hans Waldmann	2	134	JG7
Maj. Wilhelm Herget	1	54	JV44

Walter Nowotny in aircraft before takeoff.

new pilots, based in Palau. Although this was an unpopular assignment with veteran fighter pilots, Nowotny again brilliantly succeeded, earning a reputation of a first-class instructor. After that, he was given command of the very first jet-fighter unit - Kommando Nowotny - and given the momentous task of developing tactics for the use of the new jets. Major Nowotny achieved two victories on the day he died in November 1944 - a B-24 and a P-51. Those brought his total to 258 victories.

RAF Typhoon pilot John Golley recalls:

'Early in November 1944 there was a rumour going around that Nowotny, the German ace flying Me.262s, had been shot down. Nobody, as far as I was aware, was particularly excited about it, and nobody had claimed the kill. All I heard was that a Tempest squadron had got him. There was sadness rather than elation that such a great fighter pilot had been killed.'

Erich Rudorffer

- Squadron: JG 2, JG 54, JG 7
- Victories: 222
  - 136 Eastern Front

- 26 North Africa
- 60 Western Front incl. 10 4/E Bombers

Erich Rudorffer

- Total Sorties: 1000+
- Awards: Knights Cross with Oak Leaves and Swords
- Theaters: Eastern Front, Western Front, North Africa
- Combat Debut: Spring 1940, France
- Remarks: Western victories include combat over France and during the Battle of Britain. 12 Victories achieved flying the Me.262.

Rudorffer was born in Zwochau/Sachsen. He flew for Lufthansa, until two months after the beginning of World War II all pilots were transferred to the Luftwaffe. In early 1940 Rudorffer was transferred to Jagdgeschwader 2 Richthofen.

Rudorffer got his first victory over a Curtiss Hawk 75, on 14 May 1940. He scored eight more times before the capitulation of France. He flew throughout the Battle of Britain, and legend has him being pursued down Croydon High Street below rooftop level by a Hurricane. He achieved his nineteenth victory on 1 May 1941; he was then awarded the Ritterkreuz and appointed Staffelkapitän of 6./JG 2 the following month. By the end of December 1941 he had claimed 40 kills.

On 11 October 1943 Erich Rudorffer wrote history when during 17 minutes he was victorious 13 times.

In the winter of 1944, Major Rudorffer was trained on the Messerschmitt Me.262 Jet fighter. In February 1945 he was recalled to command I./ JG 7. He scored twelve victories with the Me.262, to bring his total to 222.

Detachment Kuhlmey's staff in Immola, Finland on 21 June 1944. On the right is Major Erich Rudorffer, and in the background is his wingman, Uffz. Tangermann.

His tally included 136 on the Eastern Front, 26 in North Africa and 60 on the Western Front including 10 heavy bombers.

Erich Rudorffer started out flying DC-2 and DC-3 in Australia. Later on he worked for PAN AM. In the 1980s he returned to fly for Lufthansa.

Kurt Welter

Kurt Welter was a German Luftwaffe fighter ace and the most successful Jet Expert of World War IIA flying ace or fighter ace is a military aviator credited with shooting down five or more enemy aircraft during aerial combat. He claimed a total of 63 victories achieved in only 93 combat missions. He recorded 56 victories at night, including 33

Mosquitos, and scored more aerial victories from a jet fighter aircraft than anyone else in World War II and potentially in aviation history.

Welter was born in Cologne-Lindenthal (Köln-Lindenthal) on 25 February 1916. He joined the military service of the Luftwaffe in 1934 and was trained as a pilot. He showed a strong natural ability as a pilot and was subsequently selected for flight instructor training and served many years as a flight instructor. In 1943 Welter transferred to an operational night fighter unit flying contemporary piston engine fighter aircraft. On 18 October 1944, after 40 combat missions, Welter was awarded the Knight's Cross of the Iron Cross (Ritterkreuz des Eisernen Kreuzes). In early 1945, Welter transferred to an experimental jet night fighter unit flying the Messerschmitt Me.262. On 11 March 1945 he was awarded the Knight's Cross of the Iron Cross with Oak Leaves (Ritterkreuz des Eisernen Kreuzes mit Eichenlaub) for 48 aerial victories. Welter survived the war and was killed in an accident at a railroad crossing on 7 March 1949.

Heinrich Bär

Oskar-Heinz (Heinrich) "Pritzl" Bär (25 May 1913 – 28 April 1957) was a German Luftwaffe flying ace who served throughout World War II in Europe.

Heinz Bär learned to fly gliders as a teenager. After the Hitler and the National Socialists came to power, Bär entered the German's clandestine pilot training program that would soon provide pilots for the airline Lufthansa and the air arm Luftwaffe. Bär enlisted in the Luftwaffe and following advanced training was accepted as an Non-Commissioned Officer Pilot.

As World War II began in Europe, Heinz Bär held the rank of Unteroffizer (or Corporal) with the 1. Staffel, I Gruppe of Jagdgeschwader 51 which flew the Messerschmitt Bf 109E fighters. Feldwebel (or Technical Sergeant) Bär downed his first enemy aircraft, an American-made French Armee de L' Air

Curtiss Hawk 75A fighter over Weissenberg, Germany on September 25, 1939. During the Battle of Britain, he was the Luftwaffe's top scoring NCO pilot with a total of 17 kills during that period. He had acquired 27 aerial victories by July 2, 1941 and was commissioned a Leutnant (or 2nd Lieutenant) plus awarded the Ritterkreuz (or Knight's Cross).

Leutnant Bär became the Gruppenkommandeur of IV/JG 51 as the unit transferred to the East on July 27, 1941 attached to JG 53 "Pik As", to join the invasion of the Soviet Union. Lt. Bär flew the Bf 109F during this period.

Oberleutant (1st Lieutenant) Bär was awarded the Eichenlaub (or Oak Leaves) to his Ritterkreuz following his 56th victory on August 14, 1941. On November 24, 1941, after the death of Kommodore Werner Mölders, JG 51 became the "Mölders" Geschwader. On February 16, 1942, Bär was awarded the Schwertern (or Swords) to his Ritterkreuz mit Eichenlaub plus he was promoted to Hauptmann (or Captain) after his 90th aerial victory.

Hauptmann Bär transferred to the Mediterranean Front to become the Gruppenkommandeur of I/JG 77 "Herzas" on May 1, 1942. He flew the Bf 109F and later the Bf 109G models. The strain of constant battle and knowledge of inevitable defeat of Axis forces in the Mediterranean later caused the stressed-out Bär to be relieved from command back to Germany in disgrace.

Following his recuperation, Hauptmann Bär was soon assigned to Reich's Defense duties with II/JG 1 "Oesau" to fly the heavily armed Focke-Wulf Fw 190A fighter as the Allied bombing campaign gathered momentum. He was eventually promoted to the rank of Major and the position of Gruppenkommandeur of II/JG 1. Bär gained his 200th aerial victory on April 22, 1944. On the sortie in which he downed his 200th aerial victory, Major Bär did not fly one of his own assigned Fw 190As but flew the now famous Fw 190A-7 "Red 23". Bär would be credited with 21 heavy bombers to his

Defense of the Reich tally by the end of the war.

In June 1944, Bär was promoted to Oberstleutnant (or Lieutenant Colonel) and transferred again to assume the position of Geschwader-kommodore of JG 3 "Udet".

Heinrich Bär

In January 1945, Bär became the Kommandeur of Ergänzungs-Jagdgeschwader 2, an advanced training unit for the Messerschmitt Me.262A jet pilots at Lechfeld, Germany. III/EJG 2 was soon transformed into an operational fighter unit. Bär downed 13 enemy bombers and fighters while he served with III/EJG 2. On April 23, 1945, Bär joined Generalleutnant (or Major General) Adolf Galland's Jagdverband 44, the so-called "Squadron of Aces" or "Squadron of Outcasts", for the last days of the war in Europe. When Galland was wounded, Bär took over command of the unit on April 26, 1945. With JV 44, he flew the prototype Me.262A-1a/U1 extra heavily armed with six cannon including two 20mm MG 151s, two 30mm MK 103s and two 30mm MK 108s. He downed his last three victories, all Republic P-47 Thunderbolts, with JV 44. Bär ended the war with the rank of Oberst (or full Colonel).

Postwar, Heinz Bär would eventually become an aviation consultant. In 1957, while performing aerobatics in a light plane on the anniversary date of his 200th aerial victory, Heinz Bär was killed instantly when he suddenly spun in from a low altitude.

Combat in the Me.262

In February, Bär was transferred to command the jet fighter training unit III./Ergänzungs-Jagdgeschwader 2 (EJG 2). In

Major Heinrich Bär on 21 February 1944 inspecting his 184th aerial victory 'Miss Ouachita', a Boeing B-17F of 91st Bomb Group. Bär is wearing his favourite US leather flying jacket, his wingman Warrant Officer (Oberfeldwebel) Leo Schuhmacher is standing to his right.

March, the unit was equipped with the Messerschmitt Me.262 fighter and sent into battle. Bär shot down 13 enemy aircraft, many of them heavy bombers like the B-17 and the B-24, bringing his score to 217. On 23 April, Bär transferred to the elite Jet Experten unit Jagdverband 44 (JV 44), led by Adolf Galland. On 26 April, he assumed command of the unit when Galland was wounded. Bär possibly flew his first operational sortie with JV 44 on 27 April 1945. Flying the Me.262 A-1/U5, a six MK 108 cannon prototype, he was accompanied by Major Wilhelm Herget and the non-commissioned officer NCO (Unteroffizier) Franz Köster when the trio engaged American fighters over Riem; Bär claimed one aerial victory.

While not flying operationally, Bär spent most of his time giving hasty instruction to the new pilots still being assigned to JV 44. With JV 44, he achieved his final four aerial victories (3 P-47s and 1 Mosquito) on 28 April, bringing his total to 220. All told, he had achieved 16 victories in the Me.262, making him the second most successful Jet Expert of the war, which he finished as a Lieutenant Colonel (Oberstleutnant).

During the final days of the Second World War in Europe, Lieutenant General (Generalleutnant) Adolf Galland attempted to surrender JV 44 to American forces from his hospital bed. At the same time Air General (General der Flieger) Karl Koller had ordered JV 44 to relocate to Prague and continue fighting. Bär, as a Galland loyalist, attempted to ignore the order. Bär was further pressured to relocate JV 44 when Major General (Generalmajor) Dietrich Peltz, commander of IX. Fliegerkorps, and Colonel Hajo Herrmann, commander of 9. Flieger-Division (J), unexpectedly emerged at the control room in Maxglan on 2 May 1945. A heated and violent dispute erupted between Bär, Peltz and Herrmann, witnessed by Walter Krupinski. He later recalled that Bär responded with "Yes, sir, but we are under the command of Generalleutnant Galland, and I will only follow orders of Generalleutnant Galland!"—a final act of disobedience that Krupinski believed could have gotten Bär shot for insubordination.

In the early morning hours of 4 May 1945, Bär gathered the pilots of JV 44 for a final briefing. Bär ordered the remaining Me.262 destroyed before going into captivity and interrogation by US Intelligence officers of the 1st Tactical Air Force's Air Prisoner of War Interrogation Unit, based at Heidelberg.

Walter Schuck

Walter Schuck (born 20 July 1920) is a former German World War II fighter ace who served in the Luftwaffe from 1937 until the end of World War II on 8 May 1945. He was born in Frankenholz, Saarland. Serving with Jagdgeschwader 5 on the Arctic front and Jagdgeschwader 7 in North Western Europe, he claimed 206 enemy aircraft shot down in over 500 combat missions plus up to another 30 unconfirmed victories. He claimed eight confirmed victories with the Me.262.

Schuck's father, a coal miner and veteran of World War I, gave his son the advice to take every opportunity to avoid service in the infantry. Subsequently Schuck voluntarily joined the Luftwaffe at the age of 16.

After leaving JG 5 Oberleutnant Schuck was trained on the Messerschmitt Me.262 Jet fighter and in early March 1945 was asked by Geschwaderkommodore Theodor Weissenberger to join JG 7. His maiden flight on the Me.262 was on 20 March 1945. After a few more familiarizing flights on the Me.262, Schuck and another pilot took off on 24 March 1945 to familiarize themselves with the high altitude characteristics of the aircraft. Cruising at an altitude of 10,000 metres (33,000 ft.), flight control informed them of enemy fighters in the vicinity. Schuck immediately set course for the enemy formation and spotted one P-38 Lightning and two P-51 Mustang fighters. In the resulting combat Schuck shot down the two P-51 fighters but the P-38 Lightning escaped.

After Hans Waldmann was killed in a flying accident, Weissenberger appointed Schuck Staffelkapitän of the 3 Staffel on 26 March. On 10 April 1945 he claimed four B-17 Flying Fortresses shot down. One of the bombers was "Henn's Revenge" of the 303rd Bombardment Group, and another was "Moonlight Mission" of the 457th Bombardment Group. Shortly afterwards, his Me.262 was hit by a P-51 Mustang of the fighter escort, piloted by Lt. Joseph Anthony Peterburs of the 55th Fighter Squadron, 20th Fighter Group Schuck having to bail out. Schuck

Walter Schuck

sprained both ankles upon landing and the war ended before he recovered.

In 2005 Schuck met Peterburs in person during a visit to the US.

Adolf Galland

Adolf Galland

When historians speak of pilots and the history of air combat, certain names invariably come up sooner. Galland was the youngest general grade officer of either side in World War II, and at age 29 he was more competent in aerial combat, strategy and tactics than many of the experts nearly twice his age. Galland fought a hard battle against his superiors on the ground, which made the danger in the air inviting, almost welcome. Adolf Hitler and Luftwaffe Chief Hermann Göring, who were always trying to find fault and place the blame on others for their own failures, began pointing fingers at the fighter pilots. Was it not they who failed to stop the death and destruction delivered by Allied bombers? Was it not the fighter pilots who demanded more of the resources and new technology, yet produced the least results? Göring betrayed his pilots and publicly denounced them as cowards, provoking the Fighters' Revolt in January 1945.

Galland, well known and admired by his enemies across the English Channel as an honorable and loyal rival, found an enemy he could not vanquish. The supreme warrior was engaged in heated battle with absolutist politicians and demagogues, who considered honor and chivalry a weakness. He eventually returned to where he had risen, the cockpit of a fighter plane, but as a lieutenant general leading a squadron. As a fighter pilot he was credited with 104 aerial victories.

Adolf "Dolfo" Joseph Ferdinand Galland (19 March 1912 – 9 February 1996)[2] was a German Luftwaffe General and flying ace who served throughout World War II in Europe. He flew 705 combat missions, and fought on the Western front and in Defence of the Reich. On four occasions he survived being shot down, and he was credited with 104 aerial victories, all of them against the Western Allies.

From 1943 to 1944, Allied bombing of Germany became more and more common. It was up to Galland to create some form of fighter base to attack the incoming bombers so that they did not reach their destination. His plan was to create an elite force of 1000 fighter pilots whose sole task would be to confront the Allied bombers. However, his plan did not come to fruition as D-Day in June 1944 and the Battle of the Ardennes (Battle of the Bulge) absorbed what rapidly dwindling resources he had at his disposal. His fighter planes were also fighting against the Mustang – a fighter that could cover much greater distances than

Bruno Loerzer (left), Galland (right) and Hermann Göring (centre), September 1940

was the norm for a fighter but a plane that could still be highly maneuverable and pack a fearsome punch. Hitler's desire to see the Me.262 used as a fighter-bomber – and a lack of fuel for these revolutionary planes – meant that these planes were not used as Galland would have wanted them used – as a pure fighter plane.

Galland openly criticised Goering for the situation the Luftwaffe had found itself to be in. In January 1945, Galland was relieved of his command and placed under house arrest. He was replaced by Gordon Gollob.

He was allowed to return to active service and in March 1945, he was given the task of setting up JV 44 – an elite group of fighter pilots. On April 26th1945, Galland was injured when he crash-landed his Me.262.

Adolf Galland ended World War Two with 103 credited kills after flying 703 missions. Seven of these kills came about flying the Me.262. He was awarded the Knight's Cross with diamonds, swords and oak leaves.

Galland Quotes

"I would like to mention that I have flown the 262 first in May '43. At this time, the aircraft was completely secret. I first knew of the existence of this aircraft only early in '42 - even in my position. This aircraft didn't have any priority in design or production."

"If we would have had the 262 at our disposal - even with all the delays - if we could have had in '44, ah, let's say three hundred operational, that day we could have stopped the American daytime bombing offensive, that's for sure."

"It's unbelievable what one squadron of twelve aircraft did to tip the balance."

"Many pilots of the time were the opinion that a fighter pilot in a closed cockpit was an impossible thing, because you should smell the enemy. You could smell them because of the oil they were burning."

“Nine g’s is good, if the pilot can stand it. We couldn’t stand it. Not in the airplanes of World War II.”

“Of course, the outcome of the war would not have been changed. The war was lost perhaps, when it was started. At least it was lost in the winter of ‘42, in Russia.”

“The throttles could only move very, very slowly, always watching the temperature, always watching. And even in throttling back, you could bust it, even being very careful.”

“This would only come if you have a revolutionary change in technology like the jet brought about.”

“We had at our disposal the first operational jet, which superseded by at least 150 knots the fastest American and English fighters. This was a unique situation.”

“We have built a total of about 1250 of this aircraft, but only fifty were allowed to be used as fighters - as interceptors. And out of this fifty, there were never more than 25 operational. So we had only a very, very few.”

“When I was fired from my post as General of the Fighter Arm, I was to give proof that this jet was a superior fighter. And that’s when we did it. I think we did it.”

ME.262 MECHANICS

Landing gear

The tricycle landing gear is fully retractable by means of hydraulic actuating cylinders. The main landing gear assembly is hinged to a built up steel box structure which is part of the major wing assembly.

The steel box structure is located between the main and auxiliary wing spars.

The main wheels rotate up and into the fuselage bottom. A valve is actuated after the wheels retract which causes the landing gear fairing doors to close. Fair the wheel opening and also function as an up-lock. A single cantilever strut 26" long of forged steel carries each main landing gear. A torque link of forged steel permits 20" travel.

A 1200psi hydraulic system actuates the landing gear. The actuating cylinder is bolted to a hinged fitting to the root rib at the end of the front spar of the landing gear torque box. The piston of the actuating cylinder is attached to the front of the shock strut.

The nose gear retracts aft and up into to the wheel well

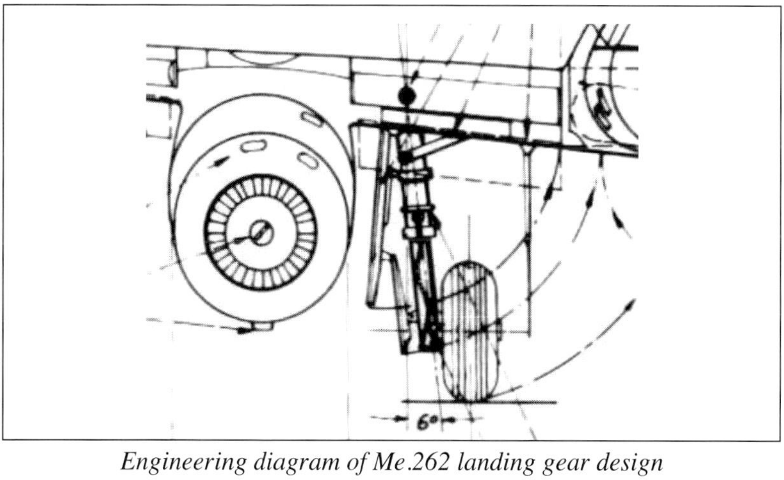

Engineering diagram of Me.262 landing gear design

compartment. A linkage closes the nose gear doors. Either a torque link or a shimmy damper was provided to eliminate shimmy action.

[Shimmy is an oscillation in aircraft landing gear that can occur both on landing and take-off, typically in a band of velocities. It causes excessive wear on components and can cause accidents. The nose wheel is roughly like a caster on a shopping trolley: the horizontal axle of the wheel is mounted in an assembly that is free to rotate about a vertical axis. Shimmy is (or at least includes) oscillation of the wheel assembly about this vertical axis. The current engineering approach has little understanding of the physical mechanisms causing shimmy, but relies on the use of shimmy dampers, and on systematic maintenance and replacement of landing gear components.]

Hydraulic system

The hydraulic system is a medium pressure type, being 1200psi for normal operation the system supplies motive force to operate the retractable landing gear and wing flaps. An engine driven hydraulic pressure pump supplies the hydraulic power. The wing flaps and landing gear are operative by means of manually operated position selector valves. The system also operated the hydraulic brakes fitted to the landed gear. A manually operated hydraulic brake was fitted to the nose gear. The hydraulic brakes on the main landing gear operated by the pilots toe action of the rudder pedals.

The brakes may all be applied simultaneously or individually. The inner main

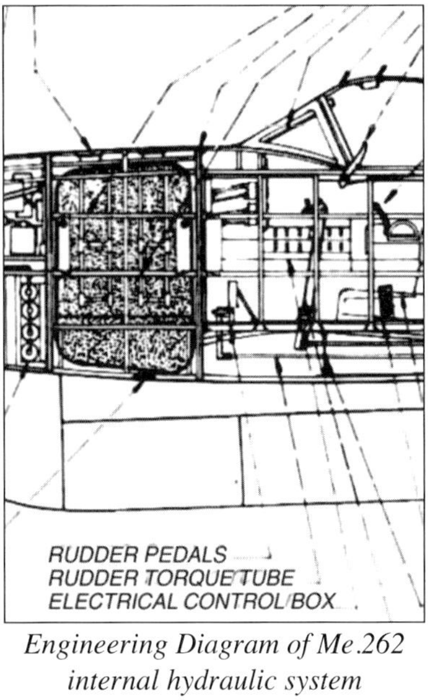

Engineering Diagram of Me.262 internal hydraulic system

wheel well doors are also operated off the hydraulic system. The pressure pump is driven by the left Turbo-Jet engine. The pressure is maintained by electric-magnetic pressure regulator.

Emergency System

Emergency extension of the landing gear and wing flaps is accomplished by means of a pneumatic system. Air pressure functions to energize the system. The operation is controlled by a magnetic solenoid valve.

[Pneumatics are similar to hydraulics with one major difference: instead of fluid, pneumatics use gas (usually air). Air is pulled into a compressor and is then forced through lines to different tools. The compressed air actuates pistons and shafts and forces them to move.]

Air Induction System

The inducted air flows into the nose cowling of each turbo-jet engine and then into the compressor.

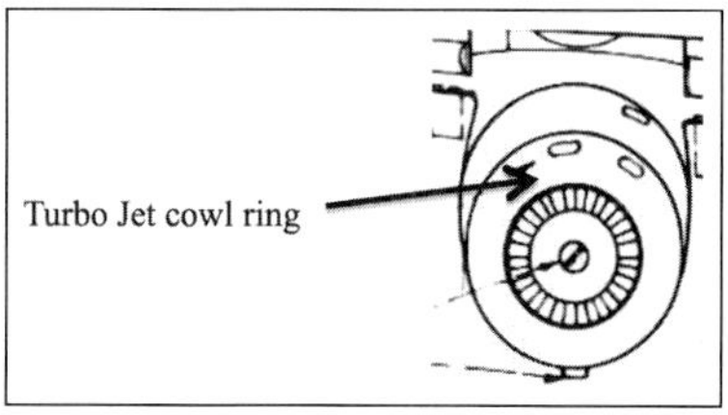

Air Deducted System

The combusted air exhaust flows from the combustion chambers through the turbine and educts from the tail pipe.

Turbo Jet Engine Controls

The amount of thrust energy developed by the Turbo-jet engine is in direct proportion to the fuel which is supplied to the burners. The Engine throttles are mounted on the left side of the cockpit. The throttle movement is fore and aft. The aft position shutting off the fuel.

Turbo Jet mount

The engine is mounted on three absorbing fittings. The right and left fittings are are attached to a horizontal member which in turn is attached to a structural nose ribs in the leading edge of the wings. The aft mounting is on the front wing spar.

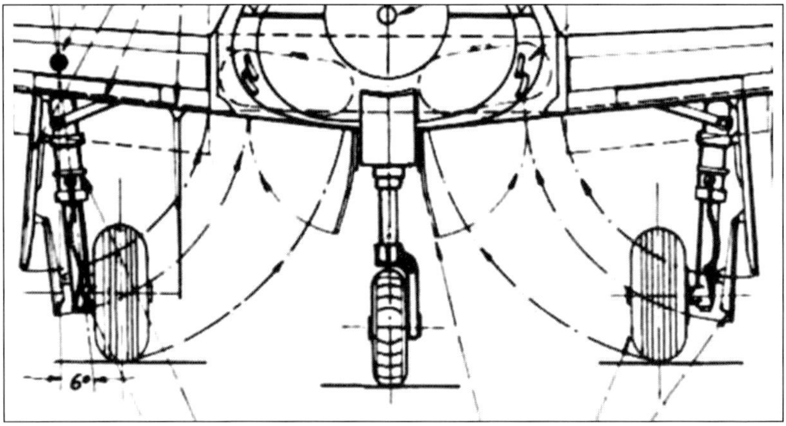

Engineering diagram of Me.262 landing gear design

Main Landing Gear Wheels

The wheel assembly consists of an 840 x 300 mm tyre and tube. The wheel assembly compromises two parts which are bolted together to facilitate quick tyre changing. The brakes are an expanding band type. The when assembly is mounted on the axe; with a set of roller bearings on each side, The tyres are inflated to 70lbs psi and are low pressure treading casing.

Electrical and Mechanical Components

Fuel System

The fuel system consists of the following major components:

- Front main cell- 240 gallons
- Front Aux cell – 204 gallons
- Rear Aux cell - 53
- Electrical fuel pumps – 158 gallons
- Fuel lines and check valves
- Fuel shut-off valve
- Fuel Quantity Indicator
- Electrical Fuel boosting pumps

The fuel cells are self-sealing. The outer shell was a fire resistant plywood. Each cell has two fuel booster pumps. The reserve fuel cell has one by means of the fuel selector valves, fuel can be pumped from any tank to either engine. Fuel can also

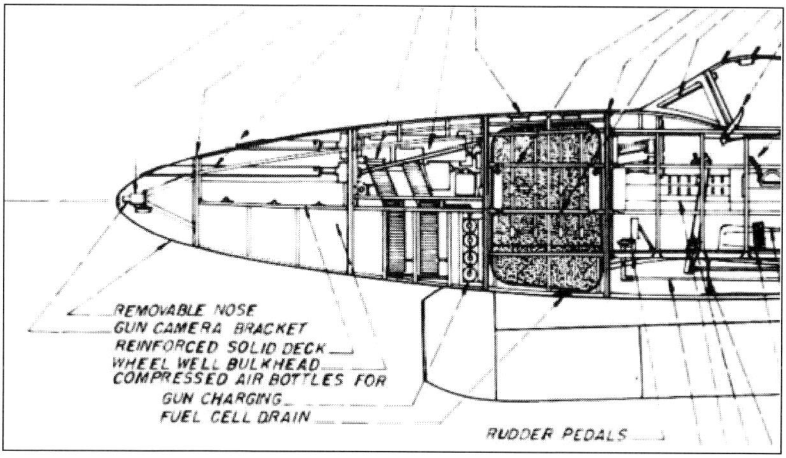

Engineering Diagram of Me.262 fueling system

be transferred from the aft cells to the forward cells purposes of longitudinal trim. Access panels permit the fuel cells to be maintained or replaced. The two fuel valves controlling the fuel flow have 3 settings on a notched quadrant. Two throttle control engine speed.

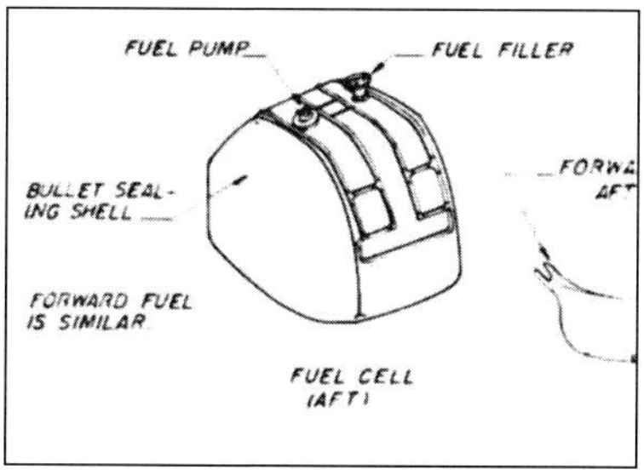

Fuel cell (aft)

Engine Oil System

An Engine Lubricating oil tank of 2.5-gallon capacity carries the oil. Two engine-driven oil pumps transfer oil to the compressor bearings, the accessory drive gears and other moving parts. A spate electrical oil pump supplied oil to the aft compressor bearings and turbine bearings.

Instrumentation

The main instrument panel is divided into two sections, the flight instruments are located on the left panel and the engine instruments being located on the right panel.

Flight Instruments

- Artificial horizon • Bank and turn indicator

- Air speed indicator • Altimeter • Rate of climb indicator
- Repeater compass • Blind approach indicator
- Radio Compass

Engine Instruments

- Engine tachometers (2)
- Tail pipe gas temperature thermometer
- Fuel injection pressure indicators (2)
- Fuel quantity indicator • Fuel consumption counters
- Free air temperature bulb selector
- Free air temperature thermometer
- Hydraulic pressure indicator

Pilot's controls

- Ventilating control • Breathing oxygen control valve
- Breathing oxygen indicator and flowmeter
- Fuel shut off and selector valves • Engine throttles (2)
- Emergency landing gear control
- Emergency wing flap control • Bomb release
- Nose wheel brake and wheel brakes

Position indicators

- Horizontal stabilizer trim • Left main landing gear
- Right main landing gear • Rudder trim tab

Electrical Controls

- Fuel transfer pump (2) • Radio FU-G-16
- Radio FU-G-25A • Recognition lights
- Pilot heater • Horizontal Stabilizer trim
- Inverter Switch • Tight and left Generators
- Storage batteries • Right and left fuel manifold drains
- Radio control box • Right and left Reidel starters
- Right and left tachometer range • Headphone volume control
- Flare release • Windshield heater switch • Navigation lights
- Directional finder • Cannon firing switch

The main electrical switch box was located on the left side of the pilots cockpit.

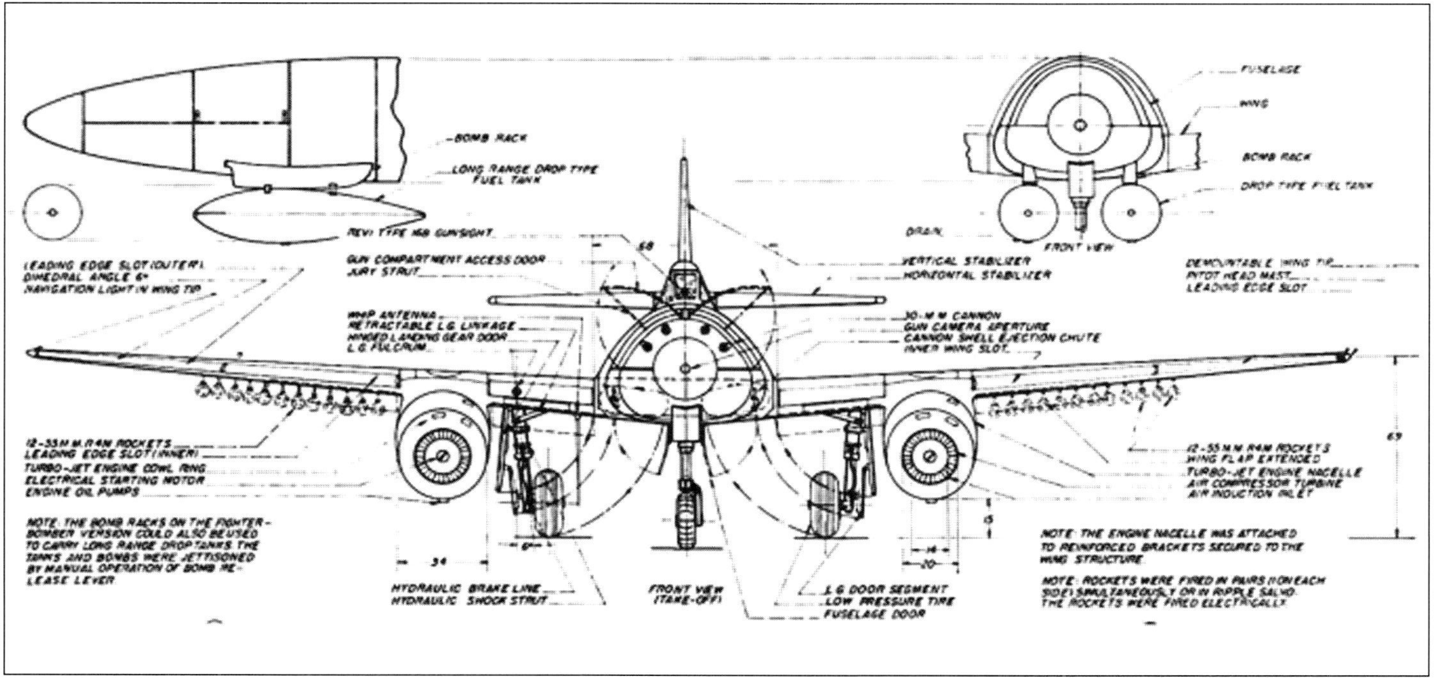

Engineering diagram of Me.262 front view

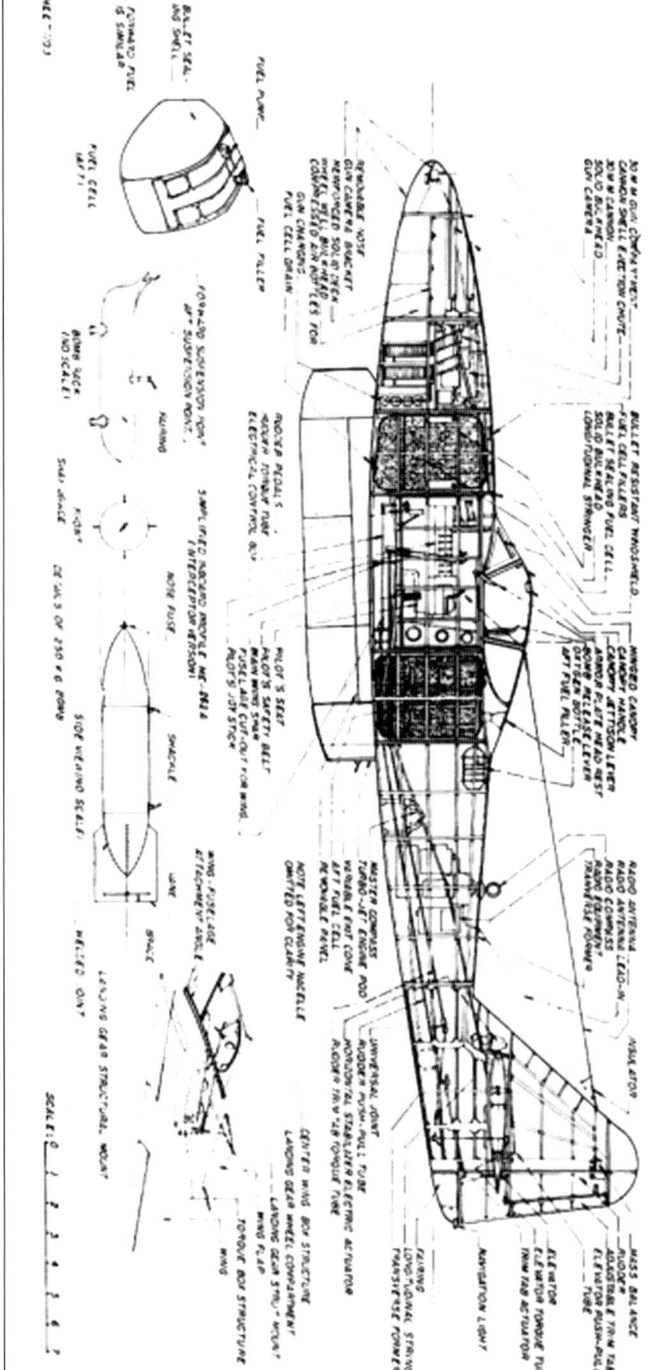

Engineering diagram of Me.262 side view

262 Ammunition/Armament

- Gun: (Me.262A-1A) four 30mm MK108 cannons (two with 100 rounds, two with 80 rounds) (Me.262B-2A) some equipped with one 50mm MK114 cannon.
- Stations: Two external hard points.
- Air to Air Missile: None
- Air to Surface missile: None
- Bomb: (Me.262A-2A) up to two 1,100lb (500kg) bombs
- Other: (Me.262A-1B) up to 24 55mm R4M Rockets (ME.262B-2A) up to 48 55mm R4M Rockets

R4M

The R4M was developed in order to deal with the increasing weight of anti-bomber weapons being deployed by Luftwaffe fighters, its manufacturers Heber AG, created one of the most successful German Air missiles, but was only fitted on a small number of planes, mostly the Me.262s and the ground attack version of the FW 109s, which mounted them on small wooden racks under the wings.

- Caliber: 55 mm
- Weight: 3.85 kg
- Weight: 0.52 kg bombs tear
- Total length: 812 mm
- Propellant mass: 0.815 kg
- Max.speed: 525 m/s
- Margin stabilizers: (8 pieces) 242 mm

Missiles were mounted on racks under the wings of Me.262 “Schwalbe”. Me262 rule carries 24 missiles R4 / M (12 pieces in one growing under each wing). By March 1945, so armed with about 60 aircraft Me262, 6 of which was marked even after 48 pc missiles.

The 55mm R4M Orkan (Hurricane) folding fin missile was a formidable weapon fitted to Me.262s late in the war. Twenty-Four R4Ms were mounted on special wooden racks mounted

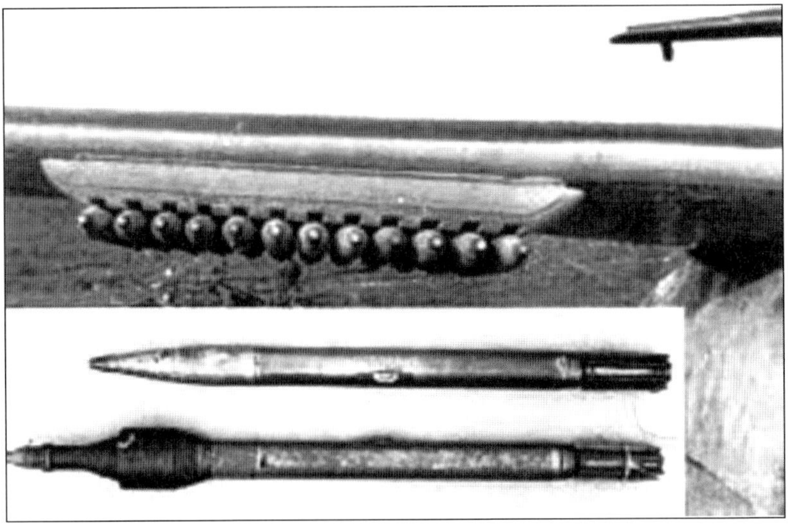

Image showing R4M placement under Me.262 wing

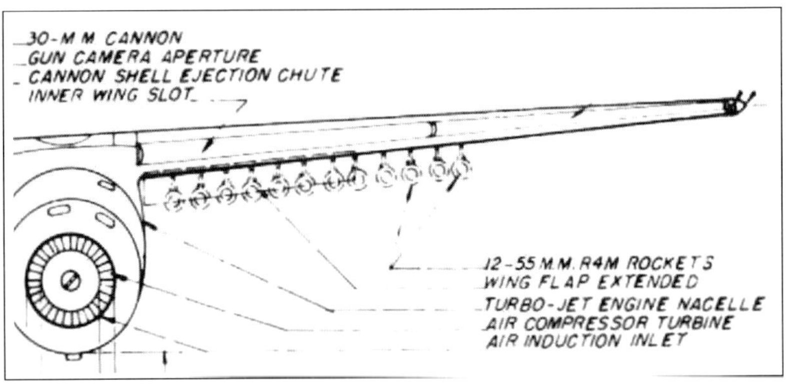

Me.262, R4M ammunition layout diagram

under the wings. Each rack held twelve missiles, which were about 2 ft. 8 ins., long and weighed 8.8 lbs. When fired, the missile traveled up to 1,700 ft./sec and packed a 1.1 lb. impact fused warhead. The warhead was typically white with the rest of the body and fins being a gray or dark metallic color.

The R4Ms were usually fired in four salvos of six missiles each at intervals of 0.07 seconds from a range of 600 meters. The R4M was unguided and the pilot simply used the usual Revi gunsite for aiming. When launched, the spring loaded fins would unfolded rearward. This enabled the R4M to be extremely compact until fired when the fins unfolded to provide stabilization. Seven of the fins were kept folded in place with a spring steel wire. The eighth fin then folded to hold the wire in place. When loaded from back to front in the launcher, the eighth

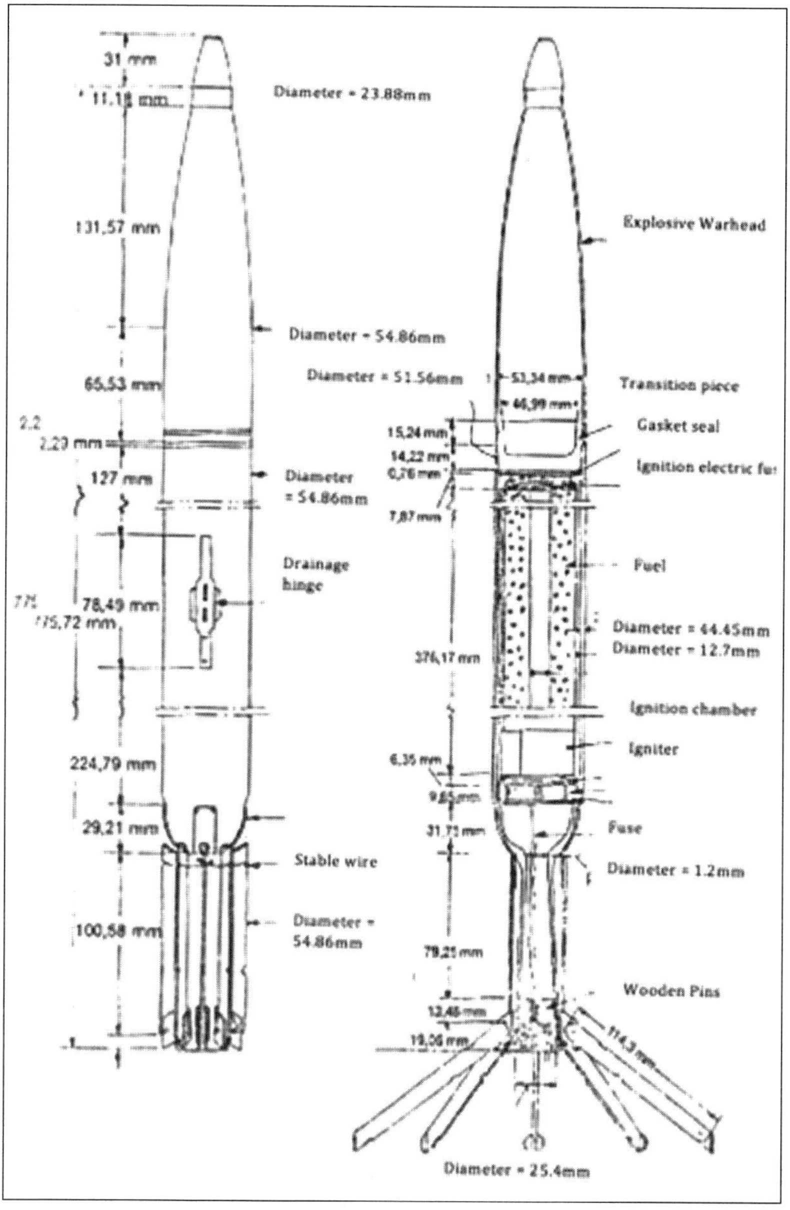

R4M air missile diagram

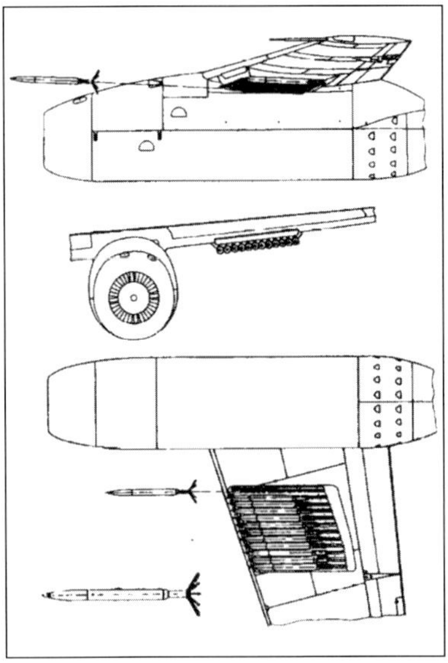

Me.262, R4M ammunition layout diagram

(top) fin was kept in place by the launch rail. Once free of the rail when fired, the top fin would spring free and release the other seven fins.

The launchers were aimed with a slight upward angle of 8 degrees. When the rockets were fired from a range of 600 meters, they had the same ballistics as the Mk 108 cannons. The warhead was a 55 mm HE shell filled with Hexogen. A single hit was all that was needed to bring down a four-engined bomber.

Only a small number of aircraft were fitted with R4M Me.262, Me 163, Ba 349 when used operationally, this weapon achieved remarkable results in March 1945 six Me.262 armed with the R4M missile system, flying out from Oberammergau intercepted an enemy bomber formation and reportedly shot down 14 B-17s. In another mission in April 1945 Me.262 armed with the R4M missile system were reported to have shot down thirty B-17s at a cost of three Me.262

Mk 108 gun

- Manufacturer: Rheinmetall-Borsig
- Caliber: 30mm/1.18”
- Length: 1057 mm/3’5.6”
- Weight: 58kg/127.9lbs
- Rounds/Minute: 660 (this rate was improved later to 850)
- Muzzle Velocity: 500-540m
- Projectile weight: 330g 0.73lbs
- Cartridge Weight: 480g/1.05lb

The MK 108 was a 30 mm caliber auto cannon manufactured in Germany during World War II by Rheinmetall-Borsig for use in aircraft.

In many ways, the Rheinmetall-Borsig MK 108 30mm cannon was considered to be a masterpiece of weapons engineering, due to it's compact size, ease of manufacture and hitting power. Although it was first designed by Rheinmetall-Borsig in 1940 as a private venture, the design was finalized in 1942. It met a later RLM requirement for a new aircraft cannon that could knock down enemy bombers with the lowest expenditure of ammunition and stay beyond the range of enemy defensive fire.

In short, the MK 108 was a blowback operated, rear-seared, belt fed 30 mm cannon using electric ignition and was charged and triggered by simple compressed air. One drawback was that once installed, there was no method to adjust the gun's harmonization. One distinctive physical feature was the very short gun barrel, which gave the MK 108 a low muzzle velocity of 500-540 meters (1640-1770 feet) per second. The maximum rate of fire was 650 rounds per minute. The operating sequence for the MK 108 went like this:

- An ammunition can fed the rounds to the gun by means of a disintegrating belt
- Once the sear was released, the bolt went forward under the action of the two driving springs
- A projection on the top of the bolt passed through the ring, thus extracting a round
- This then forced the round into the chamber and fired the round while the heavy bolt was still moving forwards
- The empty cartridge case reinserted itself in its link after firing
- Ejection was achieved by means of pawls activated by camming grooves that were cut into the top of the bolt
- Finally, the new round slipped into position and the

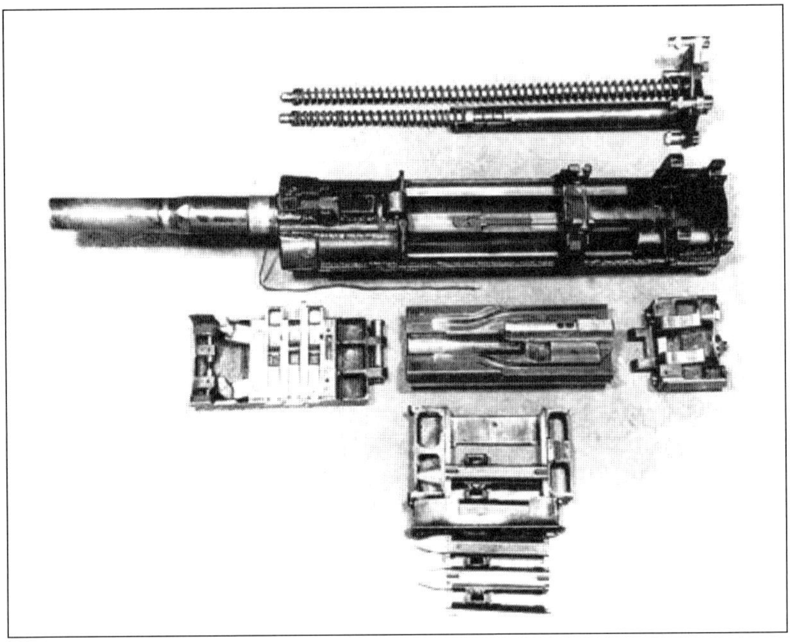

MK108 30mm cannon

sequence repeated.

An interesting feature was that neither the barrel or receiver moved in recoil, the entire force of firing was absorbed by the rearward movement of the bolt against the driving springs, which buffered against the recoil. No locking mechanism was needed, because by the time the fired round had overcome the inertia of the firing bolt, the round had left the barrel and the pressure had dropped.

JUMO 004

Specifications

- Number of combustion chambers: 6
- Fuel: kerosene
- Rate of airflow: 19,5 kg/s
- Compression: 3,5:1
- Thrust: 900 kp
- Max. Rotational speed: 8700 u/min
- Weight: 750 kg

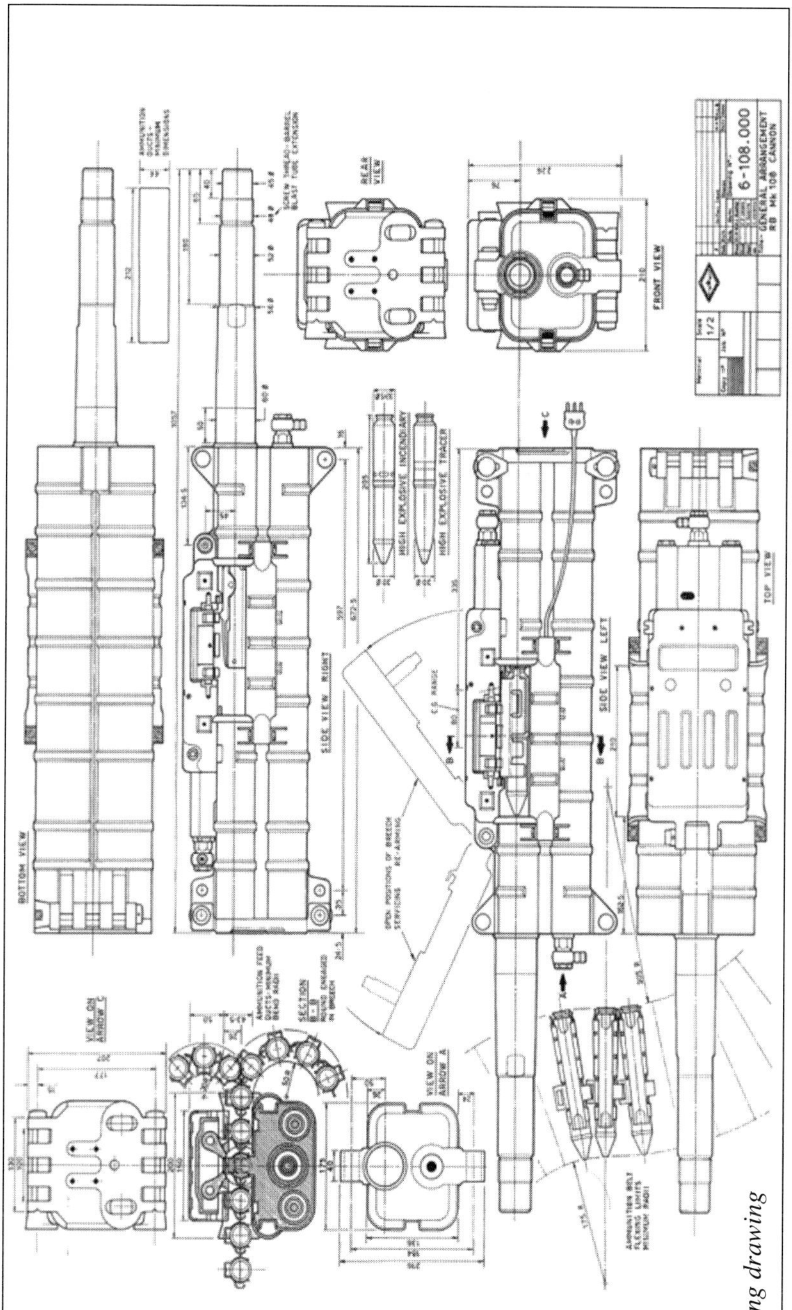

MK 108
engineering drawing

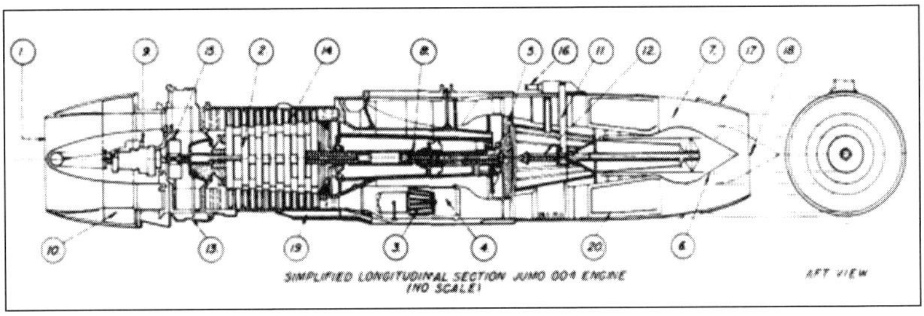

Jumo 004 engineering drawing

1. Air induction 2. Axial air compressor 3. Fuel spray 4. Combustion burner 5. Turbine rotor 6.Variable exit cone 7. Tail pipe 8. Turbine drive shaft 9. Reidel engine starter 10. Starting fuel tank (annular) 11. Variable exit cone drive 12. Screw drive jack shaft 13.Engine oil pump 14. Stator blade 15. Accessory drive 16. Servo motor drive shaft 17. Cooling air pick-up 18. Air eduction 19. Air cooling shroud 20. Cooling air baffles

- Diameter: 800 mm
- Length: 3800 mm

Engine characteristics

Operating cycle: air intake – compression – combustion – gas expansion – exhaust thrust

- The “Riedel-starter” is a small two-stroke engine situated inside the intake cone fairing, which could be started electrically or manually.
- The eight-level axle-compressor consists of a rotor with runner blades and a stator with fixed guiding blades.
- The compressed air is mixed with fuel and the mixture is ignited in the so called combustion chambers (6) at approximately 2.000”C.
- The hot gases produced by the combustion are mixed with feed air and cooled down in order not to damage the turbine blades.
- The turbine is driven by the thrust of the hot exhaust gases producing a rotation that serves to build up the compression in the axial compressor.
- The nozzle needle regulates the passing amounts of exhaust gases automatically by changing the ring shaped exhaust

pipe.

The first preproduction series was the Jumo 004A-0. This engine was used for extensive flight tests, which were not satisfactory due to material overload and failure of the fan blades.

The Jumo 004 would prove to be the source of the Me.262's greatest weakness. The turbojet was at this time still in its infancy and many technological hurdles had to be overcome. This resulted in a lengthy period of development, which led to continued delay in the development, and production of the Me.262. One of the problems was that the materials necessary for proper heat proofing were extremely rare in war-torn Germany. Alternate materials had to be used which resulted in engines that were less than reliable. In some cases, a brand new engine would suffer catastrophic failure during initial run-up. Even engines that worked right had a very short operational life. Most would only last for 12 hours of operation. On many occasions, pilots were forced to land with one or both engines out.

The Jumo 004 had six combustor cans arranged around the central casting. This casting carried the rear compressor bearing and the turbine shaft bearing. Three cans carried spark plugs. The engine was designed to run on diesel fuel. The approach to combustor design was to have a flame chamber region in the combustor for primary combustion at a close-to-stoichiometric

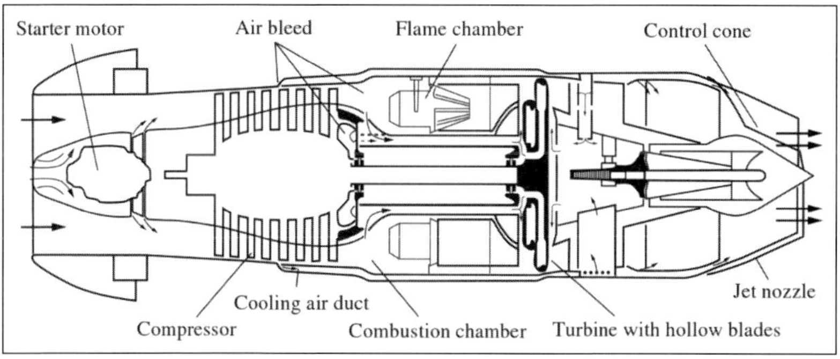

Jumo 004 internal engine. drawing and description

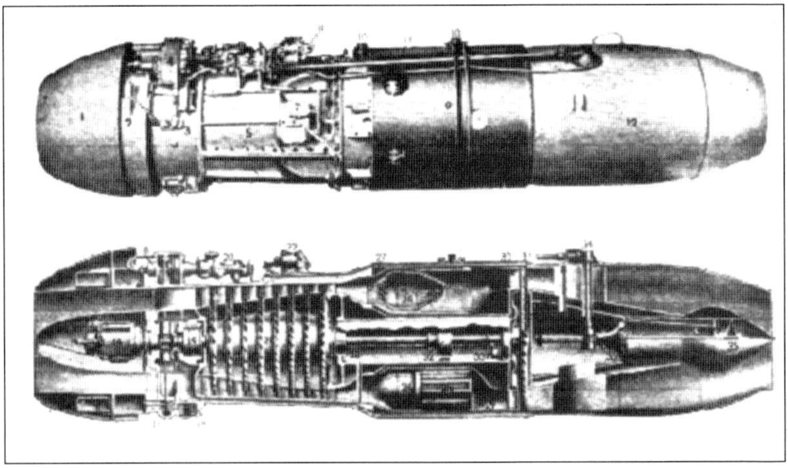

Jumo 004

ratio. To obtain good mixing and a short flame length, the primary combustion air was introduced in this chamber with swirl, and fuel was injected with a swirl against the airflow. The combustion chambers were made of aluminized sheet steel.

The Me.262 began as a preliminary design in 1939 and the first prototype flew in 1941, not with a turbojet engine, but with a 700hp Jumo 210G piston engine. It was not until 1942 that the Messerschmitt Me.262 was fitted with two Junkers Jumo 004 turbojet engines, and after a series of test flights, this new German fighter was finally introduced in 1944. Its maximum speed was 560 mph.

"Franz had started with just a few key people, and as he was unable, under the Reich's labor priority system, to hire engineers from the already hard pressed piston engine community, he was forced to take new engineers, just graduated from school, and press them into service. It was not until 1944 that the entire jet division grew to more than 500 people." Walter Boyne

A young German physicist, Hans Von Ohain, was in the forefront. He started by working on his own at Gottingen University. He then went to work for Ernst Heinkel, a plane-builder who had a strong interest in advanced engines. Together they crafted the world's first jet plane, the experimental Heinkel He 178, which first flew on August 27, 1939.

Building on this work, the German engine designer Anselm Franz developed an engine suitable for use in a jet fighter. This airplane, the Me.262, was built by the firm of Messerschmitt. It was the only jet fighter to fly in combat during World War II. But the Me.262 spent most of its time on the ground because it used too much fuel. It was a sitting duck for Allied attacks.

With the airframe of the Me.262, the Junkers Jumo 004 axial flow gas turbine jet power plant is a compromise between design desire and available materials and production facilities. Outstanding evidence of compromises resulting from lack of materials is the fact that more than 7% of the air taken in is bled off for cooling purposes. Despite this, however, most engines were found to have a service life of about only 10 hr. against a "design life" of 25 – 35 hr. Additional compromises are evident in the design, which shows that the production engineer – undoubtedly hampered by lack of both plant facilities and

Two Jumo 004 engines powered the Me.262.

adequate skilled labor – has been as important a factor in its construction as was the designer.

But the Germans had made real progress in overcoming materials difficulties, for just after they capitulated that development of a new alloy of excellent resistant qualities had made it possible to get up to 150 hr. service in actual flight tests, and up to 500 hr. on the test stand.

COCKPIT DIAGRAMS - INSIDE THE 262

Swept wings had been proposed as early as 1935 by Adolf Busemann, and Messerschmitt had researched the topic from 1940. In April 1941, he proposed fitting a 35° swept wing (Pfeilflügel II, literally "arrow wing II") to the Me.262, the same wing sweep angle that would later be used on both the American F-86 Sabre and Soviet MiG-15 Fagot fighter jets. Though this was not implemented, he continued with the projected HG II and HG III (Hochgeschwindigkeit, "high speed") derivatives in 1944, which were designed with a 35° and 45° wing sweep, respectively.

Interest in high-speed flight, which led him to initiate work on swept wings starting in 1940, is evident from the advanced developments Messerschmitt had on his drawing board in 1944. While the Me.262 HG I actually flight tested in 1944 had only small changes compared to combat aircraft, most notably a low-profile canopy (tried as the Rennkabine (literally "racing cabin") on the Me.262 V9 prototype for a short time) to reduce drag, the HG II and HG III designs were far more radical. The projected HG II combined the low-drag canopy with a 35° wing sweep and a butterfly tail. The HG III had a conventional tail, but a 45° wing sweep and turbines embedded in the wing roots.

Messerschmitt also conducted a series of flight tests with the series production Me.262. In dive tests, it was determined that the Me.262 went out of control in a dive at Mach 0.86, and that higher Mach numbers would lead to a nose-down trim that could

Me.262 interior

not be countered by the pilot. The resulting steepening of the dive would lead to even higher speeds and disintegration of the airframe due to excessive negative g loads.

The HG series of Me.262 derivatives was estimated to be capable of reaching transonic Mach numbers in level flight, with the top speed of the HG III being projected as Mach 0.96 at 6,000 m (20,000 ft) altitude. Despite the necessity to gain experience in high-speed flight for the HG II and III designs, Messerschmitt undertook no attempts to exceed the Mach 0.86

INSTRUMENTAL PANEL COCKPIT ME.262
1. Air speed indicator 2. Flight indicator 3. Rate of climb indicator 4. Altimeter 5. Radio 6. Ammunition counter switch 7. Tachometers 8. Tailpipe gas temperature indicator 9. Fuel injection pressure gauge 10. Fuel Gauges 11. Cockpit heat control 12. Fuel Counters 13. Free air temp. bulb selector 14. Photo-observer switch 15. Free air temp gauge 16. Hydraulic pressure 17. Nose wheel brake 18. Ventilator Control

limit for the Me.262.

The Me. 262 was to be further developed to increase range, with drop tanks, better fuel, and a built-in Walther Rocket unit in the fuselage to increase climbing speed. More armament was to be built in and more armor was to be fitted for protection in attacking bomber formations.

After the war, the Royal Aircraft Establishment, at that time one of the leading institutions in high-speed research, re-tested the Me.262 to help with British attempts at exceeding Mach 1. The RAE achieved speeds of up to Mach 0.84 and confirmed the results from the Messerschmitt dive tests. Similar tests were run by the Soviets. No attempts were made to exceed the Mach limit established by Messerschmitt.

After Willy Messerschmitt's death, the former Me.262 pilot Hans Guido Mutke claimed to be the first person to exceed Mach 1, on 9 April 1945 in a Me.262 in a "straight-down" 90°

dive. This claim is disputed because it is only based on Mutke's memory of the incident, which recalls effects other Me.262 pilots observed below the speed of sound at high indicated airspeed, but with no altitude reading required to determine the actual speed. Furthermore, the pitot tube used to measure airspeed in aircraft can give falsely elevated readings as the pressure builds up inside the tube at high speeds. Finally, the Me.262 wing had only a slight sweep incorporated for trim (center of gravity) reasons and likely would have suffered structural failure due to divergence at high transonic speeds. One airframe (Me.262 HG1 V9, Werknummer 130 004, with Stammkennzeichen of VI+AD) was prepared with the low-profile Rennkabine racing canopy and may have achieved an unofficial record speed for a turbojet-powered aircraft of 975 km/h (606 mph), altitude unspecified.

LEFT HAND SIDE FORWARD ME.262 COCKPIT

1. Operating handle- emergency landing gear systems
2. Operating handle- emergency flap lowering systems
3. Horizontal stabilizer trim control lever
4. Horizontal stabilizer trim indicator
5. Position indicator- left main gear 6. Position indicator – nose gear
7. Position Indicator – right main gear 8. Breathing oxygen control valve
9. Throttle controls 10. Fuel shut off and selector valves
11. Rudder trim control 12. Rudder trim tab position indicator
13. Breathing oxygen indicator and flow meter

LEFT HAND SIDE COCKPIT ME.262

1. Circuit breaker 2. Flap control push buttons
3. Landing gear control push-buttons 4. Compressed air pressure gauge
5. Position indicator – left main gear 6. Position Indicator – nose gear
7. Position Indicator – Right main gear

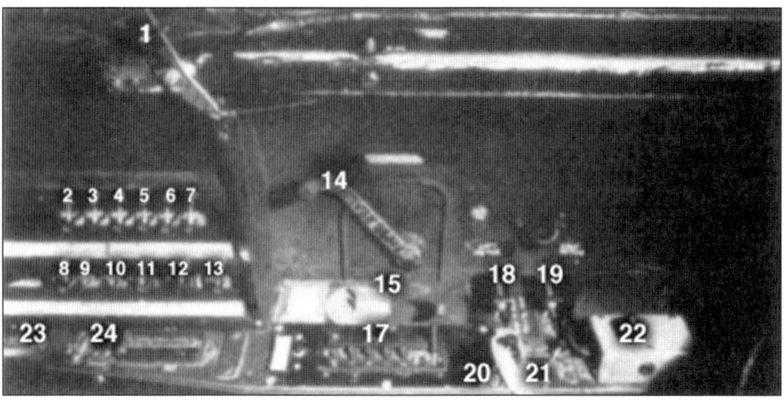

RIGHT HAND SIDE COCKPIT ME.262

1. Canopy release lever 2. Fuel transfer pumps switch 3. Fuel pump switch
4. Fuel pump switch 5. Radio-switch- Fu G 16 6. Radio-switch – Fu G 25a
7. Recognition lights switch 8. Pilot heat switch 9. Stabilizer control switch
10. Inverter control switch 11. L.H generator switch
12. R.H generator switch 13.Battery switch 14. Bomb release handle
15. L.H fuel manifold drain 16. R.H fuel manifold drain
17. Radio control box – BC-602-A 18. L.H Riedel starter switch
19 R.H Riedel started switch 20. L.H tachometer range button
21. R.H tachometer range button 22. Earphone volume control
23. Windshield heater switch 24. Flare release switch

COMMENTS, SOURCES, & REVISION HISTORY

The story that the Me.262 could have made a major difference in the war if not for Hitler's insistence that it be built as a fighter-bomber seems to exist in a fuzzy state between myth and fact. Most recent documents on the Me.262 suggest that the teething problems with the Jumo-004 engines were really the critical path for aircraft development, and though Hitler's insistence on development of the aircraft as a "Jabo" led to a bureaucratic fiasco, it's hard to prove that it made all that much difference in practice.

In fact, some authors have suggested that the idea of using the Me.262 in the "Jabo" role was not stupid at all. Hitler felt, with good reason in November 1943 that existing aircraft types could deal with Allied bombers. His major concern was to be able to deal with Allied amphibious landings on the beachhead where they were most vulnerable, and if there had been substantial quantities of jet bombers available that could have penetrated the thick fighter screen over the Normandy beachhead, they might have made all the difference. Who can say now?

The Me.262 might have changed the course of the war or lengthened it, if not for the fact that the useful life of the engines was measured in only a dozen or so hours. Compare that to today's engines which run for tens of thousands of hours and continue to be reliable. The jet engine was such a new concept that its reliability was affected by a lack of refined metals, and production was slowed by the bombing and chaos preceding the coming defeat of Germany. Nevertheless, the Me.262 struck fear in the hearts of U.S. Army Air Forces bomber crews. The sight of a 540 mph fighter slicing through bomber formations when U.S. escort fighters could not match its speed left observers in awe. Certainly Germany lost the war because it was outnumbered, the aircraft was difficult to build and it had notoriously unreliable engines, the aircraft's production rating is low - so too is its service record, having only been active for a little over two years. But its aviation technology inspired design staffs in America and elsewhere after the war to enter the jet age in deadly earnest.

The Me.262 will forever be in the record books as being the world's first fully operational jet fighter - a legend of the skies and the seventh greatest fighter of all time and influencing the designs of post-war aircraft such as the North American F-86 Sabre and Boeing B-47 Stratojet.

MORE FROM THE SAME SERIES

Most books from the 'Luftwaffe in Combat 1939-1945' series are edited and endorsed by Emmy Award winning film maker and military historian Bob Carruthers, producer of Discovery Channel's Line of Fire and Weapons of War and BBC's Both Sides of the Line. Long experience and strong editorial control gives the military history enthusiast the ability to buy with confidence. The series advisor is David McWhinnie, producer of the acclaimed Battlefield series for Discovery Channel. David and Bob have co-produced books and films with a wide variety of the UK's leading historians including Professor John Erickson and Dr David Chandler.
Where possible the books draw on rare primary sources to give the military enthusiast new insights into a fascinating subject.

Voices from the Luftwaffe

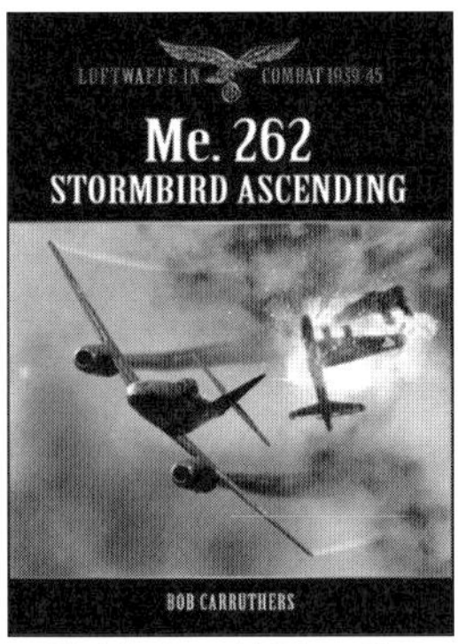

Me.262 - Stormbird Ascending

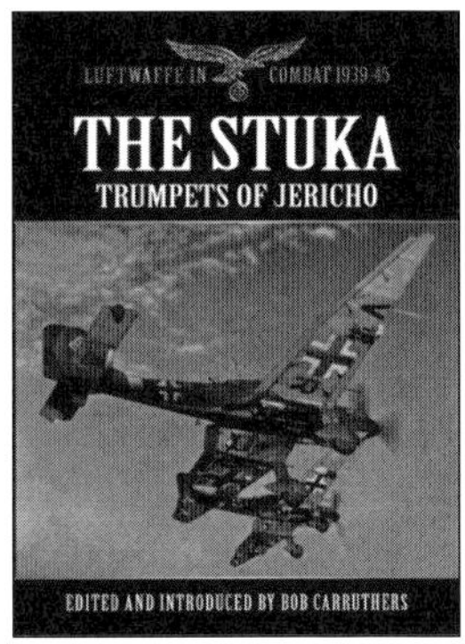

The Stuka - Trumpets of Jericho

Luftwaffe Combat Reports

Der Adler -
The English Language Editions

For more information visit www.pen-and-sword.co.uk